When Your Child Has LD*

(Learning Differences)

A Survival Guide for Parents

Gary Fisher, Ph.D.
and Rhoda Cummings, Ed.D.

Edited by Pamela Espeland
Illustrated by Caroline Price Schwert

free Spirit®

PUBLISHING

Library of Congress Cataloging-in-Publication Data
Fisher, Gary L.
    When your child has LD (learning differences) : a survival guide for parents / Gary Fisher, Rhoda Cummings ; edited by Pamela Espeland.
        p.   cm.
    On t.p. "LD" is followed by an asterisk.
    Includes bibliographical references and index.
    ISBN 0-915793-87-3 (pbk.: alk. paper)
    1. Learning disabled children—Education—United States—Handbooks, manuals, etc. I. Cummings, Rhoda Woods. II. Espeland, Pamela, 1951–   . III. Title.
LC4705.F58 1995
371.91—dc20   95-5583
                                                                          CIP

10 9 8 7 6 5 4 3 2 1
Printed in the United States of America
Cover and book design by MacLean & Tuminelly
Index compiled by Eileen Quam and Theresa Wolner

Portions of this book have been adapted from *The Survival Guide for Kids with LD*, *The School Survival Guide for Kids with LD*, and *The Survival Guide for Teenagers with LD* by Rhoda Cummings, Ed.D., and Gary Fisher, Ph.D. (Free Spirit Publishing, 1990, 1991, 1993). The list of children's books in the Resources has been adapted from *Understanding LD (Learning Differences): A Curriculum to Promote LD Awareness, Self-Esteem, and Coping Skills in Students Ages 8–13* by Susan McMurchie, M.A. (Free Spirit Publishing, 1994).

With a few exceptions, the names of the people portrayed in this book have been changed to protect their privacy.

Free Spirit Publishing Inc.
400 First Avenue North, Suite 616
Minneapolis, MN 55401-1730
(612) 338-2068

DEDICATION

To Gary's parents, Dick and Eunice Fisher,
and to Rhoda's parents, Lloyd and Madge Woods.

ACKNOWLEDGMENTS

A book such as this is not only the product of the authors, editor, and publisher, but also of the many kids with LD and their parents we have encountered over the years. They have inspired us and taught us.

We especially want to acknowledge Lynette Carroll, R.J. and Debbie Johns, Jo Anne Krumpe, and Jill Mustacchio, who graciously contributed their thoughts and feelings for inclusion in this book. A very special thanks to Arlene Morton for generously sharing her experiences.

Thanks also go to Cheri Dunning, friend and repairer of impaired formats and phrases.

Finally, we are grateful to our families—Debbie, Colin, and Aaron and Carter and Courtney—for the many opportunities and challenges they provide to us.

CONTENTS

Introduction

"I know now that success is not measured by academic achievement; there is so much more to all of us and everyday I am reminded of the uniqueness and importance of the individual. Who are we to judge what is normal? There is no normal. Each of us is on our own journey. I wouldn't trade this journey with my son for anything."

Parent of a third grader

Since you are reading this book, it's safe to assume that you are a parent whose child has LD. Perhaps your child has been labeled "learning disabled" by the school or by professionals such as psychologists, physicians, or speech therapists. Or perhaps you suspect that your child has a learning disability, based on information you have read or heard from others. You're probably wondering what a learning disability is and what it means for your child. You may be concerned about how it will affect your child's school performance and future.

When Your Child Has LD: A Survival Guide for Parents is meant to inform you, reassure you, and help you to help your child—and yourself. You'll gain a better understanding of learning disabilities, the rights you have if your child is identified as having LD, specific ways to help your child, and what you might expect as your child progresses through school and into adulthood. But before we get into the whats and the how-tos, we want to explain what we mean when we use the term "LD."

We *don't* mean "learning disabled" or "learning disabilities." We mean "learning different" or "learning differences." This is the language we used in our first three books, written for young people—*The Survival Guide for Kids with LD, The School Survival Guide for Kids with LD,* and *The Survival Guide for Teenagers with*

1

LD—and it is the language we use in the rest of this book as well. While "disability" has negative connotations for many people, "difference" is more positive, accepting, and accurate. We all have differences. We all learn in our own unique ways. Some people are good at academic subjects; others are good at learning other things.

Children who are identified as having LD may have difficulties in school but can easily master nonacademic information and skills. For example, Gary did very well in school, earning high grades in academic subjects. However, in junior high he had to take woodshop and make a lamp. When he plugged in his lamp, he blew all the fuses in the shop. Eric, in contrast, had a hard time with reading. There were no LD classes when he was a student, but he would certainly be identified as having LD if he were in school today. A few years ago, Gary bought a lawn mower that needed some assembly. According to the instructions, assembly would require about one hour. After struggling for three hours, Gary called Eric to come over and help. Almost immediately, Eric noticed that Gary had put several parts on the wrong sides of the lawn mower.

Gary and Eric learn differently. Gary learns academic material easily and has difficulty with mechanical tasks; Eric is just the opposite. Each learns in his own way.

While we cannot ignore the importance of doing well in academic areas in a modern society, we feel that it is incorrect to assume that something is "wrong" with children who learn academic material differently than most other children. If your child has been identified as having LD, he or she is *not* retarded, "dumb," or "slow."

"My son creates and builds things. He's great with pulleys and gadgets. One time he made a space ship that was powered by energy from the sun."

Parent of a ninth grader

"There is so much more to my daughter than her academic ability. She possesses a whole array of talent and strengths. The school she attends acknowledges this and encourages her full potential."

Parent of an eighth grader

"I found out about a program called the Talent Academy within our school district. I signed Marcus up for it. He goes every Friday to a mechanical drawing class. His regular classroom teacher lets him teach the class what he has learned. The program has allowed Marcus to contribute rather than always receiving help."

Parent of a sixth grader

"Music is my son's outlet to express his talent. His peers accept him in high regard."

Parent of a tenth grader

However, you also need to understand that learning differences are usually not temporary and normally can't be "cured." Through learning from others, patience, and effort, Gary can perform some mechanical tasks, but they are not easy for him. His friend Eric still struggles with reading as an adult. Many children who are identified as having LD become competent in some academic areas but not in others. Reading, spelling, and arithmetic can be especially difficult for them.

What determines how well a child with LD will succeed? There are many factors, including the type of LD the child has, the quality of instruction in school, the child's personal motivation and effort—and especially the patience, support, and encouragement of parents and teachers. In other words, *you* can make a big difference in your child's success, now and in the future.

We hope this book will inspire you, guide you, and answer your questions about LD and your child. One of the most rewarding results of writing our first three books has been the many letters we have received from young readers, parents, and teachers. We'd like to hear from you, too. Let us know how our book helped you, and please share your ideas for making it better. Write to us at this address:

Gary Fisher and Rhoda Cummings
c/o Free Spirit Publishing Inc.
400 First Avenue North, Suite 616
Minneapolis, MN 55401-1730

Best wishes for you and your child,

Gary Fisher and Rhoda Cummings
Reno, Nevada

~~~~~~~~~~~~~~~~~~~~~~~~

Parents Speak Out about Their Gripes and Concerns

When we asked parents of children with LD to share their greatest gripes, here is what they said:

1. People think that my child is stupid.

2. Some teachers don't understand LD. They call my child "lazy" or "unmotivated."

3. No one seems to be able to explain LD to me, tell me what causes it, or give me any idea of what to expect in the future.

4. The school has made a lot of promises about my child's progress and the services my child would receive, but those promises haven't been kept.

5. I can't get specific suggestions from the school for helping my child.

6. My child works as hard as he can and still gets poor grades. He feels discouraged and I feel frustrated.

7. When I met with the school personnel about my child, they used a lot of big words with no explanations. I didn't understand what they were talking about.

8. People blame me for my child's LD. They ask, "Did you use drugs while you were pregnant?"

9. Whenever I mention that my daughter is LD to an acquaintance, friend, or relative, I hear about a "cure" that someone read about or saw on TV. It makes me feel guilty that I don't know about and try these things.

When we asked parents to share their concerns about their children, here is what we heard:

1. Will my child have the education and skills needed to compete with others for jobs?

2. Having a child with LD creates a lot of stress in our family. How will this affect our other children—and our marriage?

3. I often wonder if my child will be independent as an adult. Will he have a job, friends, and a spouse?

4. Considering how hard my child struggles with school, it's hard for me to imagine her in college. In today's world, how can she succeed without a college education?

5. My child seems so vulnerable. How can I protect him against the possibility of exploitation and abuse?

6. My child is frustrated so much of the time. How will this affect her self-esteem now and in the future?

7. How can I help my child get along better with others—peers, teachers, family members?

You may have similar complaints and concerns. In this book, you'll find information and suggestions that will help you to help your child—and feel better about yourself.

1

What Is LD?

~~~~~~~~~~~~~~~~~~~~~

Five Facts about LD

1. LD and dyslexia are not the same. Not all kids with LD have difficulty reading.

2. Kids with LD are not dumb. In fact, some are gifted.

3. Kids with LD may go to college. Many do.

4. Kids with LD aren't "doomed" to low-paying, dead-end jobs. Many can and do get good jobs and enjoy successful and interesting careers

5. Some kids have mild learning differences, while others have learning differences that are more pronounced or profound. LD is a range on a continuum. Each individual child with LD has unique abilities and difficulties.

~~~~~~~~~~~~~~~~~~~~~

When we say "LD," we mean "learning different" or "learning differences" because we believe that everyone learns in his or her own way. However, this is not what everyone means when they use that term. As a parent, you need to know what school personnel and other professionals may mean when they say "LD." You also need to understand that there are various types of LD.

There is no universal agreement among professionals about LD and what it means, so you may read or hear in other places information that is different from what you will find here. Please be reassured that the knowledge, advice, and tips in this book have been gathered from several reputable sources and from our own experience studying, counseling, and teaching children with LD and working with their families and teachers.

One Definition of LD

The Individuals with Disabilities Education Act (IDEA) of 1991 is a federal law that includes definitions of all "handicapping conditions" that enable children to receive special education services. (Although we don't like the term "handicapping conditions," it is the term used in special education legislation.) One handicapping condition is "specific learning disability," which is defined as follows:

> "'Specific learning disability' means a disorder in one or more of the basic psychological processes involved in understanding or in using language, spoken or written, which may manifest itself in an imperfect ability to listen, think, speak, read, write, spell, or to do mathematical calculations. The term includes such conditions as perceptual handicaps, brain injury, minimal brain dysfunction, dyslexia, and developmental aphasia. The term does not include children who have learning problems which are primarily the result of visual, hearing or motor handicaps, of mental retardation, of emotional disturbance, or of environmental, cultural, or economic disadvantages." *Federal Register*.

If this definition is confusing to you, you're not alone. In simpler language, it means that a child with LD has difficulty in some area of learning in school that *is not* the result of poor vision or hearing, or of a condition such as cerebral palsy, emotional disturbance, or mental retardation. Also, the child's learning difficulties *cannot* be due to being poor, or to differences between the child's culture and that of most other children in the United States, such as coming from a home where English is not the primary language.

Each state develops its own rules to determine if children are eligible for special education services. Usually, one of these rules has to do with a discrepancy between "predicted" and "actual" academic achievement. For example, Sam is given an intelligence test and scores in the average range for children his age. From this, we would predict that Sam would be able to learn academic subjects in school at an average rate. If Sam is doing average work in arithmetic but his reading is far below average, there is a discrepancy between his predicted and actual academic achievement in reading. To educators, a discrepancy like this acts as a "red flag," indicating that Sam might have LD.

To greatly simplify the definition of LD given in IDEA, we might say this:

> "'LD' means that a child is not achieving at the expected level in at least one academic area. This is not due to a vision or hearing problem, a motor problem like cerebral palsy, mental retardation, a serious emotional problem, poverty, or cultural differences."

Right now you might be thinking, "That's fine—now the definition isn't so confusing—but it still doesn't tell me why *my* child is not performing at the expected level." You're absolutely right. In Chapter 2, you'll find information that will help you to better understand your child's LD. In order to communicate with your child's teachers and other school professionals, however, it's important to have some understanding of the language they use everyday.

Five Types of LD

From the way many people use the term "LD," it's easy to assume that everyone who has LD is exactly alike. Articles about LD in newspapers and magazines and programs on television create the impression that every child with LD has the same characteristics. In fact, nothing could be further from the truth. There are at least five different types of LD. As you read the descriptions that follow, keep in mind that your child may have characteristics of more than one type. And even within types, individual children have learning differences.

1. "Academic Learning Disability"

Children with academic LD have difficulty learning one or more academic subjects, but they normally perform well in other areas such as art, music, athletics, or mechanics. Quite often, the children have a hard time with some aspect of reading. Difficulty with reading is identified fairly quickly by parents and teachers because reading is so important in school and is one of the first subjects children are taught.

However, it is possible for children with academic LD to be good readers and have difficulty with other school subjects, such as arithmetic. Similarly, they may find it hard to comprehend one aspect of reading, such as phonics, but be able to understand quite well what they read.

Although children with academic LD can certainly have a great deal of difficulty in school, they often find an area of success as they get older. We worked with a young man named Steve who had academic LD which affected his reading. Although Steve struggled in school, he was a gifted artist. Steve was recognized for his talent in high school, won a scholarship to an art college, and is now a successful commercial artist.

2. "Language Learning Disability"

Children with language LD may have difficulty understanding what others say to them ("receptive language"), or they may have trouble saying what they mean ("expressive language"). This affects their ability to learn in school, since they may have a hard time understanding instructions or making themselves understood by others, including their teachers. There are also social consequences, since language is critical in our interactions with others.

Because this kind of LD is so obvious, children who have it are frequently thought to be unintelligent, and other children (and some adults) may make fun of them.

Gary was once asked to test a six-year-old named Rontain. Rontain didn't seem to understand instructions in class and hardly ever talked. His teacher suspected that he was mentally retarded. Gary found that Rontain had a serious language learning difference, but on tests of non-verbal problem-solving—such as putting blocks together to match abstract designs—Rontain scored well above average. Once the test results became part of his school records and Rontain's teachers learned that he wasn't retarded, they encouraged him to use his talents. He did exceptionally well in geometry, architecture, and mechanical drawing.

3. "Attention Deficit Disorder"

There is a tremendous amount of information currently available about attention deficit disorder. This term actually applies to two conditions: *attention deficit hyperactivity disorder* (ADHD), and *attention deficit disorder without hyperactivity* (ADD). Most of the information in the popular press concerns ADHD.

Children with ADHD may have trouble sitting still, concentrating on their school work, paying attention in class, and blocking out distractions. They are often impulsive, saying and doing things without thinking of the consequences.

The difference between ADHD and ADD is that ADHD children are extremely motor-active. They always seem to be "on the go."

Not all children with attention deficits are classified as having LD. Some are able to learn academic subjects as well as or better than other children. However, many children with attention deficits do have LD. Their difficulty in concentrating and their distractibility results in poor academic progress. To understand attention deficits, imagine yourself reading a book somewhere in your house. Meanwhile, the dog in the yard next door is barking. You are able to "tune out" the noisy dog and continue your reading. Children with attention deficits cannot tune out visual or auditory stimuli. As a result, it is hard for them to accomplish many tasks that require them to pay attention.

Since there are several special issues for parents who have children with attention deficits, we suggest that you read a book specifically on this topic. Following are three titles we know and recommend:

▶ *Hyperactivity: Why Won't My Child Pay Attention?* by S. Goldstein and M. Goldstein (New York: John Wiley and Sons, Inc., 1993).

▶ *Helping Your Hyperactive–Attention Deficit Child*, 2nd rev. ed., by J.F. Taylor (Roseville, CA: Prima Publishing, 1994).

▶ *Parent's Guide to Attention Deficit Disorders* by L.J. Bain (New York: Dell, 1991).

4. "Perceptual Motor Disability"

Children with this type of LD have trouble using a pen or pencil and have difficulty copying material from the chalkboard or from a book. Their handwriting may be messy and illegible. Often these children are not proficient at games and sports that require coordination and quick reflexes.

5. "Social Perceptual Disability"

Frowning, crossing your arms, and turning your back are non-verbal ways people use to communicate displeasure or to indicate that they don't want to be around a particular person. In contrast, smiling and facing someone means that you are interested in having an interaction with that person. Some children have difficulty interpreting the nonverbal cues that people use to show what they are thinking and feeling. This type of LD causes social challenges for children.

Why We Don't Use the Term "Dyslexia"

As a psychologist, Gary is often asked by parents and teachers to test children for "dyslexia." There have been many newspaper and magazine articles and television shows about dyslexia. You may have read about or watched programs about people who see words and letters backwards, yet somehow have managed to compensate at school and on the job.

The term originated in medical literature and suggests that there is something in the brain that prevents an individual from learning to read. Early literature in this field also used terms such as "congenital word blindness," "strephosymbolia," and "minimal brain dysfunction."

There are three reasons why we try to avoid using the term "dyslexia." First, it alarms parents, especially those who have previously received inaccurate information about dyslexia. Many children have trouble remembering the correct names for letters that appear and sound similar, such as "b," "d," and "p." They may confuse these letters when they write words. In fact, it is quite normal for this confusion to continue through age eight. But very few children with LD past this age are unable to see that "b" and "d" don't look the same.

Second, when a child has a hard time with reading and a parent reads or hears about "dyslexia," the parent may believe that the child has some form of brain damage. As you will read in Chapter 2, some LD may be due to differences in the brain. However, in most cases the cause of a child's reading difficulties cannot be precisely determined, and it makes no sense to spend a lot of time and money searching for physical causes.

Finally, because "dyslexia" is a medical term, it implies that something is "wrong." We prefer to focus on the learning differences children have and the best types of instruction, curriculum, and class placement for a particular child. In our experience, the term "dyslexia" is not useful in achieving these goals.

There are some cases in which medical treatment can help children learn better. For example, if a child has seizures, medication may control the seizures so they won't disrupt the child's school experience. A child with an attention deficit disorder may take medication to help him or her concentrate and pay attention. But most kids with LD need *educational* treatment, not medical treatment. That is why we avoid the use of medical terms that label children.

2

Why Does My Child Have LD?

"It's hard to get over the feeling that you as
parents have failed somewhere. You have to understand
that your child developed at a slower or different rate
than a child without LD, and it's not your fault."

Parent of an eleventh grader

"Your child learns either in slower or different stages.
It's nothing you've done. Some parents think that they
should have read to their child every night or something.
That's not the reason my child has LD."

Parent of a ninth grader

At some point in time, probably every parent whose child has
LD asks, "Why *my* child?" There are genetic and environmental factors that are associated with LD, and in this chapter we describe
some of these factors. However, we ask that you keep the following
points in mind as you read the descriptions:

1. **In most cases of LD, the cause cannot be determined.** By the
   time a child is identified as having LD, he or she is usually in
   school. No parent can remember everything that happened
   during pregnancy, birth, and early childhood. Even if there was
   a dramatic event (such as a serious head injury), a cause-and-
   effect relationship between the event and the LD can rarely be
   determined.

2. **Even if the cause of a child's LD can be determined, this usually has no impact on the educational placement and
   instructional strategies that are used with the child.** Parents
   may invest a great deal of time, money, and emotional energy
   trying to determine the cause of and cure for their child's LD.
   But learning differences can't be "cured." Instead, we need to
   determine the ways a child learns best and identify the teaching
   strategies and materials that work best with that child.

3. **Parents who search for causes and cures may feel a lot of guilt and blame.** While it is perfectly natural to experience strong emotions when you have a child with special needs, guilt and blame can be immobilizing. In Chapter 7, you'll find suggestions for dealing with these emotions. For now, try to understand that feeling guilty or assigning blame won't help you and it won't help your child.

Genetic Causes

"Nobody in our family is good at math.
My child has trouble with math. I had trouble with
math in school, and I still do. My parents were
terrible at math. Maybe there's a connection."

Parent of a third grader

"My father never really learned to read. He wasn't
illiterate—he liked to listen to books on tape—but
sitting down with a book or magazine was something
he didn't do. Now my son is having reading difficulties
in school. We tell him that he must have gotten this
from his grandfather—along with his blonde hair."

Parent of a fourth grader

As early as 1905, researchers were speculating that LD was genetically transmitted. Since that time, numerous researchers have investigated the possibility of a genetic link to LD. This type of research is very difficult to do, since there is always an interaction between genetics and environment. Sorting out which factor contributes to any human characteristic or ability is difficult, to say the least.

One way to investigate the role of genetics is to compare identical twins (who are genetically identical) and fraternal twins (who are no more similar genetically than any siblings). Researchers in the 1950s found that with identical twins, if one child had LD, so did the other in every case. With fraternal twins, both children had LD in only one-third of the cases studied. These findings seem to support a genetic explanation for LD.

It has also been found that males are much more likely to have LD than females. Although there are other possible explanations, some researchers have speculated that the LD gene is dominant in males and recessive in females. In our own work with families, we often find that parents of children with LD report a history of LD in the family, often in the males. Although this does not prove a genetic cause for LD, it does provide strong support for the idea.

There is also some logic to a genetic explanation in our concept of "learning differences." We seem to have no trouble accepting that there is some inherited ability to perform well in athletics, art, or music. Similarly, people will often laugh about the lack of these talents in families. It makes some sense to imagine that the aptitude for learning certain academic subjects, particularly when they are taught in the traditional manner, may also be inherited.

A genetic explanation for LD does not mean that a child will be unable to acquire academic skills. Just as someone can become competent at playing a musical instrument through patient, creative teaching and a great deal of practice, the same should hold true for children who have difficulty in academic areas.

Environmental Causes

Environmental causes of LD may be *prenatal* (occurring during pregnancy), *perinatal* (occurring during birth), or *postnatal* (occurring after birth).

Prenatal Causes

Certainly, events can occur during pregnancy that affect the central nervous system of the fetus. Diseases that the mother may contract, toxemia, and nutrition all have an impact on the developing fetus. There has been a great deal of attention paid recently to children who were exposed to drugs prenatally, including legal drugs such as tobacco, alcohol, and prescription drugs. While research on the impact of prenatal exposure to drugs on learning is just now occurring, it is clear that there is *no* "safe" level of tobacco, alcohol, and illegal drug use during pregnancy.

Perinatal Causes

It has long been known that children born prematurely have a higher incidence of many developmental difficulties than children born at full term. On the other hand, many premature children experience no developmental difficulties.

Problems also may occur during the birth process that reduce oxygen flow to the infant's brain, such as a breech birth or having the umbilical cord wrapped around the infant's neck. Fortunately, modern technology has reduced the frequency of such occurrences.

Accidents or injuries that happen during the birth process may result in brain damage, which seems to be related to later learning difficulties.

"From the minute she was born, I knew that something wasn't quite right. She was kind of limp. The doctor whisked her off and for two hours, I didn't see her. I didn't know what happened to her, and it was really scary."

Parent of a fourth grader

"She was a month premature and she was induced. I think that is what happened to make her have LD."

Parent of a fourth grader

Postnatal Causes

There are several postnatal factors which may cause damage to the central nervous system, including extremely high fevers with accompanying seizures, diseases such as encephalitis, or head injury from an accident. An infant who is malnourished may have slow brain growth.

Some postnatal factors may lead to a child being identified as having LD even when there is no damage to the central nervous system. For example, Maria experienced frequent ear infections as an infant and as a young child. Her hearing was affected and her language development was delayed. By the time Maria started school, her hearing was fine, but she had not acquired concepts that most other children her age had already learned, such as colors, numbers, and an understanding of "up" and "down," "over" and "under." Her listening skills were undeveloped. Maria had trouble learning and was identified early as having LD.

There are other reasons why some children may enter school without having been exposed to concepts and materials that most other children are familiar with. Perhaps the family lacked the financial means to provide this exposure. Perhaps the parents have LD, never received the help they needed in school, and don't know how to help their children. According to the federal definition of LD given in Chapter 1, these children should probably not be identified as having LD, but they frequently are placed in LD programs anyway.

3

Early Signs of LD

■□■□■□■□■□■□■□■□■

"My daughter was always kind of behind my son.
The pediatrician kept telling us everything was fine, all
kids develop differently, and I could accept that. But at
age two-and-a-half, she still wasn't speaking very well,
and she was saying only a very few words. I remember
my son talking in sentences at that age. Plus her
coordination wasn't good. Every time I took her to the
doctor, they said that she was fine, she was developing
a little bit slower but within the normal range."

Parent of a six-year-old

■□■□■□■□■□■□■□■□■

More and more, children with LD are being identified as
early as first grade. This is good, because the sooner parents and
teachers know that a child has a learning difference, the sooner
they can start helping the child. Early intervention—meaning
appropriate *educational* treatment, starting in preschool or
before—can reduce or eliminate some of the negative effects of
having a learning difference, such as falling behind in school,
being labeled "slow" by teachers and "dumb" by other children,
and developing low self-esteem.

Emerging research with children who have Down's syndrome is
showing that these mentally retarded children can make significant
gains in learning, when intervention is early and intense. For children with LD, these gains could be even more significant, since
they have *at least* average intelligence—some score in the gifted
range on intelligence tests—and they have the potential to perform
at least as well as children who don't have LD.

How is it that we identify and begin early intervention with
mentally retarded children, yet we neglect to do so with most children who have LD? You probably already know the answer.
Down's syndrome and many other disabilities, such as blindness
and deafness, are obvious from a very early age. Most parents are
made aware of these conditions when their children are born or
shortly thereafter. Almost immediately, they are referred to medical

experts and early intervention specialists, who work with them to coordinate treatment. By the time their children start school, most already have had five or six years of special help.

A learning difference is much subtler and harder to recognize. Although many children with LD experience delays in reaching the traditional developmental milestones—sitting, crawling, walking, talking—these delays are usually within the outer limits of "normal," and anxious parents are reassured by pediatricians not to worry because their son or daughter is "just a little immature" and "will catch up shortly." Most parents heed their doctor's advice and relax a bit, although many parents we know whose children have LD acknowledge that they always had a "gut feeling" that something was "wrong." Meanwhile, the children begin to sit, crawl, walk, and talk, and the parents breathe a sigh of relief. Their relief is short-lived, however, because once the children start school and begin to fall behind, the old anxieties resurface, and the parents begin the long, drawn-out process of trying to determine what lies at the bottom of their children's difficulties.

Two Case Studies

Jonathan

Jonathan is fifteen months old and just beginning to take his first steps. He sat up when he was five months old, but he didn't crawl until he was eight months old. Although Sandra, his mother, is somewhat concerned that he started walking so late, she knows that some babies who are completely normal don't walk until they are eighteen months old. Still, she is plagued with the feeling that something "isn't quite right" with her son.

Jonathan was born with the umbilical cord around his neck and was without oxygen for a brief period during delivery. The doctor kept the baby in an incubator for 24 hours after he was born but assured Sandra that everything was fine. When Jonathan was four months old, he began to experience projectile vomiting at every meal. The doctor told Sandra that her son's pyloric valve (a flap covering the entrance from the esophagus into the stomach) was underdeveloped, gave her some heavy syrup to put into his formula, and told her to feed him sitting up in his infant seat. After a while, the vomiting stopped, although Jonathan continued to be distressed and fussy at mealtimes.

For Jonathan's first birthday party, several of Sandra's friends brought their babies, all about the same age as Jonathan. The other babies were very interested in the gifts and the wrapping paper, the birthday balloons and decorations. Jonathan, however, crawled back into the bedroom and spent most of his birthday repeatedly picking up the telephone receiver and returning it to its cradle.

Jonathan is not making the babbling sounds that many of the other children his age are making. He does not seem as responsive to his environment as other toddlers, and he cries and fusses a lot. According to Sandra, Jonathan has been a challenging baby in many ways. When she expresses her concerns to the pediatrician, he tells her not to worry, that Jonathan is developing normally and should improve as he matures.

Karen

At three-and-a-half years old, Karen is driving her parents crazy. Like Jonathan, she developed physically well within the normal ranges; she took her first steps when she was only ten months old and, according to her parents, Burrus and Ramona, "she has not stopped moving since." Also like Jonathan, she has always been a fussy eater, and she has not slept all night from the day she was born.

Both Burrus and Ramona work outside the home, so Karen goes to a day care center. The director of the center says that Karen does not get along well with the other children. She won't sit down and play with them, although she tries to disrupt their play. She is restless during planned activities, and she is constantly moving.

At home, Karen rarely plays with her toys, preferring instead to engage in repetitive activities such as flipping through the pages of books, running a toy car back and forth over the same path, or frantically scribbling all over the pages of her coloring books. She seems to understand much of what she hears, but her spoken language is difficult to understand and limited to two- or three-word phrases. Ramona states that Karen cannot entertain herself for even five minutes, she never engages in pretend play, and she has no interest in commercial games.

Over the past year, Burrus and Ramona have expressed their concerns to the pediatrician, whose usual response has been, "She is probably just immature; she just needs some time to grow up." Recently, however, because of Karen's difficulties with expressive language, the doctor suggested that Burrus and Ramona might want to have Karen tested at the university speech and hearing clinic. Karen is now on the clinic's waiting list.

Do Jonathan and Karen Have LD?

Both Jonathan and Karen are still very young, but both exhibit behaviors that we believe may indicate learning differences.

Most parents and many pediatricians are not aware of these indicators. They base their decisions about a child's development on physical milestones—sitting, standing, crawling, walking. In recent years, however, early childhood specialists are being trained to look for the more subtle behavioral signs that the development of a child's cognitive (intellectual) abilities is not keeping up with his or her physical abilities.

Avoiding the "Failure Track"

"In first and second grade, everything seemed okay. In third grade, the teacher said that something wasn't right with my son. His fine motor coordination was not very good. He could learn visually but not through hearing. All I could think of was, he's halfway through grade school. Why did it take so long for someone to notice that he had a learning difference?"

Parent of a fourth grader

What happens when a child with LD starts school? For the first two or three years, the child's teachers (who may suspect the truth) may tell the parents that the child is "a little immature" and "will catch up eventually." They may advise the parents to hold the child back a grade to allow "a bit more time to mature." The parents may give in and have the child repeat the first or second grade.

For some children, this is exactly what they need, and they are able to achieve at their grade level from that point on. But for many other children, being held back is not the answer. They repeat a grade or two and still have trouble in school, with the added social issues caused by "flunking." By the time they reach the third or fourth grade, their academic difficulties have become so overwhelming that they experience more failures than successes.

The frustrated parents and teachers finally recommend that the children be tested for LD. The children are evaluated, found to have LD, placed in special education programs, and eventually start receiving the special help they need. By this time, of course, three or four years have gone by—time which could have been spent on effective educational treatment and remediation. Instead, the children are labeled "learning disabled," and the parents are more anxious than ever.

We believe that many of these difficulties might be prevented if more parents and professionals knew how to identify some of the subtle early signs of a learning difference. If parents were aware of the early signs of LD, they could advocate for their children and insist that early intervention programs be just as accessible for them as they are for other children with special learning needs. Remember that children with LD have *at least* average intelligence. With early intervention, their potential for future academic and personal success is greatly enhanced.

When It's Too Late for Early Intervention

If your child is already in school, then obviously it's too late for early intervention. But it's not too late to help your child in many other ways. (That's what the rest of this book is about.) And it's not too late for you to learn some of what the experts know about the early signs of LD. In fact, many parents we know are relieved to discover that their "gut feelings" about their children were right—there *was* something going on, even if they couldn't put a name to it.

Think back to *before* your child started school, perhaps to when he or she was in preschool. Then answer the following questions to the best of your recollection.

1. Did my child play games of pretend, alone or with others?

2. Did my child engage in symbolic play? (Example: Moving a block around the floor and pretending it's a car.)

3. Did my child start talking at around the same time as other children his or her age? Was my child speaking in sentences by age four?

4. Did my child understand cause-and-effect relationships? (Example: Seeing a broken glass and assuming, "Someone must have dropped it.")

5. Did my child play hide-and-seek? (This game requires an understanding of object permanence. Children who have this understanding realize that objects and people don't cease to exist simply because they are out of sight.)

6. Did my child demonstrate an eager and alert interest in other people and activities?

7. Was my child interested in interacting with other children his or her age?

8. Did my child seem to be behind other children his or her age in terms of physical coordination, language use, interpersonal interactions, and social activities?

9. Did my child engage in repetitive behaviors that seemed to be pointless?

10. Did my child seem overly impulsive, distractible, or too energetic—much more active than other children his or her age?

Chances are, if your child has been identified as LD, you answered "no" or "maybe not" to questions 1–7, "yes" or "maybe" to questions 8–10. These are generally considered reliable early signs that a child may have a learning difference. The next sections help you to understand why.

What We Know about Children's Intellectual Development

―――――――――――

"If only we could know what was going on in a baby's mind while observing him in action we could certainly understand everything there is to psychology."

Jean Piaget, 1927

―――――――――――

Much of what we know about the development of children's cognitive abilities is based on the work of Swiss psychologist Jean Piaget (1896–1980). Piaget spent his life observing young children and their interactions with the environment. His work and ideas have influenced educators all over the world. Today, modern computer technology is providing child development researchers with exciting new information about the structure and function of children's thought processes, much of which supports Piaget's findings and theories.

Piaget believed that the development of children's thinking abilities from birth through adolescence occurs within four distinct stages:

1. *sensorimotor* (birth through age 2),

2. *preoperations* (ages 2 through 5/6),

3. *concrete operations* (ages 5/6 through 11/12), and

4. *formal operations* (ages 11/12 through adult).

Our focus here is on the first two stages. If you want to know more about Piaget's work, we recommend the following book, which we have found to be especially helpful for parents of children with LD:

▶ *Piaget's Theory of Cognitive and Affective Development*, 4th edition, by B. Wadsworth (New York: Longman, 1989).

Piaget's sensorimotor and preoperations stages describe the normal thinking abilities of infants and preschoolers. They may help you to understand why your child behaved in certain ways, and they may reassure you that if you had a sense that something was "wrong," you were right.

Piaget's Sensorimotor Stage

During this stage, which begins at birth and lasts until age two, children take in information through their senses. They can't help but smell, hear, touch, taste, and feel everything. This is how they learn about the physical world, which is crucial for their intellectual development.

The sensorimotor stage is divided into six periods.

Period 1 (months 0-1)

▶ Most of an infant's behaviors during this period are purely reflexive—sucking, crying, grasping, wriggling, squirming.

▶ All learning takes place through the senses.

▶ There is no understanding of object permanence. If something is out of sight, it's also out of mind.

▶ There is no understanding of cause-and-effect ("If Mommy puts on her coat, she must be leaving." "If Daddy is frowning, he must be angry").

▶ There are no feelings or emotions.

▶ Infants are unable to differentiate themselves from the environment.

▶ They don't yet recognize that Mommy and Daddy are distinct and separate individuals.

Because there are no physical characteristics of LD, it is usually impossible to detect a learning difference during the child's first month of life. However, many parents of children with LD report that they knew something was different about them from the beginning. Their newborns were extremely fidgety, cried and fussed frequently, and experienced difficulties with eating.

To our knowledge, there is no research that links these early behaviors with later LD. However, there is a great deal of evidence that children with other disabilities of neurological origin (such as cerebral palsy and Down's syndrome) often have a hard time coordinating chewing, sucking, and swallowing. It seems reasonable, then, that at least *some* infants with similar difficulties will later be identified as LD, since some learning differences are believed to be due to neurological differences. Of course, many infants who have these difficulties do not turn out to have LD.

Period 2 (months 1–4)

▶ With the development of hand-eye coordination, babies can deliberately move a hand or other object to their mouth. (Many start sucking their thumbs or fists during this period.)

▶ Eye coordination enables them to follow the path of an object within their range of vision.

▶ Eye-ear coordination enables them to turn their head in response to and in the direction of a familiar sound, such as a parent's voice.

▶ They still don't understand cause-and-effect.

These behaviors are not usually recognized as developmental milestones, but they are clear indicators of a child's intellectual growth.

Period 3 (months 4–8)

▶ Babies become more interested in objects and people, which they are beginning to perceive as separate from themselves.

▶ They can coordinate their hand movements with their eye movements to grasp objects within reach.

▶ They begin to engage in goal-directed behaviors and can repeat interesting actions. (Example: Accidentally kicking a mobile, then intentionally repeating the action to make the mobile move again.)

▶ They begin to interact more actively with other people. (Example: Squealing with delight when Mommy or Daddy enters the room.)

▶ They begin to understand that objects are permanent and continue to exist even when they are out of sight.

These subtle behaviors indicate giant leaps in the development of an infant's thinking abilities. Many young children with LD will not perform these behaviors at this stage of their growth.

Period 4 (months 8–12)

During this period, babies behave in ways that indicate clear acts of intelligence.

▶ They engage in goal-directed behaviors, actually thinking about a specific goal, then initiating a sequence of behaviors to achieve it. (Examples: A child wants a toy that is behind a pillow. She mentally plans to get the toy by moving the pillow first, then grabbing the toy. Or a child notices that another child has a toy he wants. He tries to pull the toy out of the other child's hands, or he pulls a string attached to the toy.)

▶ They anticipate events by associating certain signs with actions that follow the signs. (Examples: A child sees Mommy putting on her coat and realizes that she is about to leave. Or a child scrapes his knee, sees Daddy coming with a bottle of disinfectant, and starts to cry. A younger infant won't cry until *after* the medicine is on the scrape.)

▶ They realize that objects stay the same shape and size whether they are close up, farther away, above or behind something else. (Example: A ball is round regardless of where it is.)

▶ They continue to develop an understanding of object permanence. They search for objects that disappear from sight, indicating an ability to remember the objects even when they can't be seen. (Example: If a rattle is hidden under a blanket, the child will move the blanket to get to the rattle.)

▶ Feelings now influence behavior. Children repeat behaviors associated with good feelings and avoid behaviors associated with bad feelings.

▶ They begin to have feelings of like and dislike for other people, a first sign of emerging social understandings.

These behaviors are much more varied and complex than those of a newborn. Children who don't exhibit these behaviors during this period may simply be immature, or they may have a learning difference.

Period 5 (months 12–18)

▶ Children begin to approach simple problem-solving through trial-and-error. (Examples: Playing around with a puzzle piece until it falls into place; jiggling a door knob until the door opens.)

▶ They look for objects that are hidden from view, starting in the place where they were last hidden. (Example: A parent hides a toy under a blanket. The child finds the toy. The parent then hides the toy behind a box. The child looks for the toy—under the blanket.) During this period, children can't yet play a good game of hide-and-seek because they can't think of all the different places where something might be hidden.

Period 6 (months 18–24)

▶ A remarkable transition occurs as children become increasingly able to solve a variety of problems. (Example: The child who wants a cookie from the jar on top of the counter can think through all of the steps needed to get it: pull out drawers, use them to climb up onto counter, raise lid to cookie jar, grab cookie. Unfortunately, this same problem-solving ability may not work quite as well when the toddler wants to get down!)

▶ They have a clear concept of cause-and-effect relationships.

▶ They have a complete understanding of object permanence. They can search for objects they don't see hidden and keep looking until they find the objects, using a logical method of searching. They love to play hide-and-seek.

According to Piaget, a fully developed concept of object permanence is the clearest sign that a child is ready to move on to the next stage of cognitive development: preoperations.

Piaget's Preoperations Stage

Piaget used the word "operations" to mean "logical thinking ability." A child who is preoperational doesn't perceive the world in the same logical manner as older children and adults.

There are four signs of cognitive development to look for during this period.

Deferred Imitation

Deferred imitation is simply the ability to imitate a past experience—an indication that a child's memory is developing. Children who play pat-a-cake by themselves, or who shake a finger at another child in the same way Mommy shakes her finger at them, are engaging in deferred imitation. Most children start practicing this at around age two. Children between ages three and four who don't engage in deferred imitation may have delayed cognitive development.

Symbolic Play

Symbolic play is evident in games of pretend. (Example: Zooming a block through the air and pretending it's an airplane. In the child's mind, the block becomes a symbol for the airplane.) Symbolic thinking is necessary for normal language development because language is highly symbolic. (The word "airplane" is even further removed from the real thing than a block is.)

Symbolic play is important to children's cognitive development because it gives them a way to express themselves—their thoughts, ideas, worries, and so on—before they are able to describe them in words.

Drawing

The ability to represent the world though drawings is another sign that children are learning to communicate with symbols. Very young children just scribble; as they mature, their drawings start representing things, and the older they get, the more realistic their drawings become.

Development of Spoken Language

Language is the most obvious sign of cognitive development during the preoperations stage. At around age two, children start using words as symbols to represent objects. They begin with one-word "sentences," but by age four most children have mastered the use of language and most of its grammatical rules.

The development of language during this stage is essential for young children to express their increasingly complex thinking abilities. It's also important for communicating with other children and adults, necessary for the development of social relationships.

According to Piaget, the ability to communicate through the use of symbols emerges between the ages of two and four years. Children who have not acquired these abilities by age four may have delayed intellectual development that points to future learning difficulties.

Remember Jonathan and Karen from pages 23–25? Their physical development was within the normal range, but their behaviors indicated possible differences in their intellectual development. You may want to read these pages again, in light of what you now know about Piaget's stages. Then take another look at the questions on page 27. What, if any, were the early signs that your child might have LD?

4

~~~~~~~~~~~~~~~~

Your Child's Legal Rights

"Once I found out about IDEA and my legal rights as the
parent of a daughter with LD, I felt more informed and
I became a more confident advocate for my daughter."

Parent of a 12-year-old

If your child has been labeled "learning disabled" by the
school, then he or she is entitled to certain legal rights. These rights
are designed to ensure that all children from ages 3 to 21 who are
identified as having a learning disability are provided with the education that is best for them. The law further specifies that students
with LD are entitled to certain related services such as speech therapy, counseling, and transportation if these services are necessary
for the child's educational success.

These legal rights were first guaranteed by the Education for All
Handicapped Children Act (Public Law 94-142), which was passed
in 1975. At first, the law applied only to children from ages 5 to
21. In 1991, the Individuals with Disabilities Education Act (IDEA)
extended the eligibility ages to include all children with disabilities
from birth to 21. IDEA also allows but doesn't require states to
establish criteria for determining "developmental delays" in infants
and toddlers that may predict future learning difficulties.

This chapter explains the law and what it means for school-age
children with LD. Please read it carefully! The information
included here will help you to obtain services that will benefit your
child. You'll be better prepared to advocate for your child and
more confident about speaking out.

How Children Are Identified as Having LD

Before a child can be eligible to receive special education services, he or she must first be *referred* for consideration for services. This referral may come from a teacher, a parent, or anyone else who believes that the child may have LD.

Next, the parents must be notified *in writing* by the school that their child has been referred for special education. They are asked to give written consent for their child to take a battery of tests, the results of which help to determine whether the child is actually eligible for special education services. The tests are administered by an assessment specialist such as a school psychologist, a diagnostician, or a psychometrician.

The tests may include:

▶ a test of intelligence, such as the WISC-III (Wechsler Intelligence Scales for Children, third edition) or the Stanford-Binet Scales of Intelligence;

▶ a variety of achievement tests to measure academic abilities in areas such as reading, math, and spelling;

▶ tests of language ability; and

▶ tests of coordination and motor skills.

Other informal assessment measures should also be considered, including:

▶ teacher observation,

▶ a family history, and

▶ other measures of the child's behaviors in and out of the school setting.

Based on the test and assessment results, a multidisciplinary team within the school decides whether the child is eligible for special education services. This team usually includes:

▶ the school psychologist (or whoever administered the tests),

▶ a special education teacher,

▶ the school counselor, and

▶ anyone else who may have an interest in the child's educational needs.

If it is determined that the child has LD and is eligible for special education, the parents are notified in writing and asked to attend a meeting with school personnel to design an educational program for the child. This meeting is called the "IEP meeting." If the school and parents decide that the child will begin special education, an IEP (Individualized Education Program) is developed that outlines all of the educational and related services the child is eligible to receive. We'll tell you more about the IEP later in this chapter.

Once a child is placed in special education, his or her special education program is evaluated each year through the IEP process. Every three years, the child receives a full assessment to determine whether he or she is still eligible for special education.

The Rights of Children with LD

When a child becomes eligible for special education services, he or she also becomes entitled to certain rights under IDEA, including:

▶ the assurance of a free, appropriate public education in the least restrictive educational environment;

▶ the provision for development of an individualized educational program and related services; and

▶ the provision for nondiscriminatory assessment.

A Free, Appropriate Public Education

All students with LD have the right to a free, appropriate public education. They also have the right to be educated in a regular classroom with children who do not have LD, if that is where they are likely to learn best.

Some children with LD may learn best somewhere besides the regular classroom—for example, in a resource room, where students with special needs spend part of each day; in a special education classroom; or even in a private school for kids with LD. If this is the case, the law says, then this is where they should go.

Some school personnel equate the "least restrictive environment" (LRE) concept with "mainstreaming," insisting that *all* students with LD be educated in the regular classroom. This is not an accurate interpretation. It's important for you to know that the term "mainstreaming" never even appears in either the Education for All Handicapped Children Act or IDEA. The LRE concept is intended to ensure that students with disabilities are educated in the environment *most like* the one in which nondisabled students are educated, *and* that this environment is one in which the students' educational needs are met *most appropriately.*

For some students with LD, especially those who need a lot of structure and individualized attention, the regular classroom is the *last* place where their educational needs can be met. If your child is being taught only in the regular classroom, but you know that his or her educational needs are not being met there, you may ask that your child be moved to a different educational setting, such as a resource room or a self-contained special education classroom.

Some students with LD who have trouble learning in the regular classroom may not need to go to a resource room or a special education classroom. They simply may need some extra help with their regular classroom work. If this seems to be the case with your child, you may ask that provisions be made in your child's education program for the regular classroom teacher to modify the assignments and the way lessons are presented so your child can keep up in class.

For example, if your child has trouble with reading, you may ask the teacher to modify the reading assignment by:

▶ tape-recording the content of the textbook, or ordering a version that is already on tape;

▶ asking a volunteer to read the book aloud to your child; or

▶ making a book available that includes the same content as the regular text, but written at a lower reading level.

Or, if your child has difficulty taking notes during lectures or copying assignments from the chalkboard, you may ask that the teacher:

▶ tape-record the lectures, or

▶ give your child handouts with the assignments written on them.

You may ask that these modifications be written into your child's IEP.

~~~~~~~~~~~~~~~

Some Pros and Cons of Mainstreaming

PROS

▶ Social interaction with other children

▶ No labels

▶ Most "normal" learning environment.

CONS

▶ A lot of distractions

▶ Not much individualized attention

▶ Kids with LD are sometimes teased

▶ It's sometimes hard for kids with LD to keep up with the rest of the class.

~~~~~~~~~~~~~~~

An Individualized Education Program and Related Services

All students who receive special education services must have an individualized educational program. This program is spelled out in a document called the Individualized Education Program (IEP). The IEP should be ready before the beginning of each new school year.

Your child's IEP is written by an IEP committee, which should include:

▶ a representative from the school district,

▶ your child's teacher (usually the special education teacher),

▶ you, and

▶ your child, if appropriate.

If your child is 16 or older, he or she must be invited to the IEP meeting. However, we believe that students of all ages should get involved in this important decision-making process. After all, it's their education!

If your child has just been evaluated and determined eligible for special education services, then the IEP committee should also include someone who is knowledgeable about the evaluation process and how to interpret the test results. This might be the school psychologist, testing specialist, or another individual who is familiar with your child's evaluation. Sometimes other school personnel who work with your child, such as the school counselor or the speech therapist, will be part of the IEP committee.

By law, the school must notify parents *in writing* about their child's IEP meeting. The school must make every effort to schedule the meeting at a time that is convenient for the parents. Although you are not required to attend the IEP meeting, we strongly recommend that you do. You know your child better than anyone else on the committee, and your presence and input can help to make sure that your child's educational needs will be met. If the IEP meeting is scheduled for a time when you can't attend, you may ask the school to change it to a time when you can. The school is obligated to do this. The law states that parents are equal members of the IEP committee, and their concerns about and wishes for their

children's educational programs must be given equal consideration. If you have specific educational goals and objectives for your
child's educational program, then make your wishes known and
ask that these goals and objectives be included in the IEP.

The IEP is an important document that should carefully outline
your child's educational program for the entire school year.
Sometimes IEPs are written in a hurry and important information
is left out. Although this is somewhat understandable, given the
large numbers of special education students for whom IEPs must
be written, you should insist that enough time be taken in the IEP
meeting to develop a document that addresses *all* of your child's
educational needs.

~~~~~~~~~~~~~~~~~~~

Tips for Being an Effective IEP Committee Member

As a parent of a child with LD, you have the right—and the
responsibility—to speak up for your child, to offer your opinions about your child's educational program, to ask for
changes, and even to disagree when something doesn't seem
right to you. For some parents, an IEP committee can be
intimidating. If you're at all concerned about what to expect or
what to do, the following tips can make the experience easier
for you.

1. **Think about what you want to say before you go into
    the meeting.** Write down your questions, concerns, sug-
    gestions, and ideas. Make a list of the items you want to
    be sure to cover. You may want to make copies of your
    list to give to the other committee members.

2. **Don't expect the "experts" to do all of the work or
    come up with all of the answers.** You're an expert, too—
    an expert on your child. Be ready with suggestions and
    possible solutions. Write them down and share them
    during the meeting.

3. **Stick to the point of the meeting.** You're all there for one reason: to develop an educational program that will help your child succeed in school. If you have other issues you want to discuss with your child's teacher, make an appointment to meet at another time.

4. **Avoid confrontations.** Be diplomatic, tactful, and respectful, even if you disagree with something another committee member says. Expect to be treated in the same way.

5. **Focus on what your child needs, not on what you think the school is doing wrong.** For example, instead of saying, "You shouldn't give my son as much homework as he had last year," try saying, "My son had trouble finishing his homework assignments last year, even though he spent hours every night doing homework. What can we do this year to lighten his load?"

6. **Think and talk positively.** Remember that each school year is a new beginning. Even if your child has had negative school experiences in the past, this year really can be different.

7. **Ask questions.** If there's something you don't understand, ask someone to explain it to you. Don't be put off by the jargon that many educators like to use. Say, "Excuse me, but I don't know what you mean by that phrase or description. Could you put it in different words?"

8. **Listen carefully and take notes.** Review your notes after the meeting. If there's something you don't understand or want to know more about, follow up with a phone call to one or more committee members.

What Your Child's IEP Should Include

An IEP is an official document that can be several pages in length. It may include special language, abbreviations, and terms with which many parents are not familiar. It helps to know what to look for in your child's IEP. Although each IEP will be unique, reflecting the individual student's abilities and needs, your child's IEP should include all or most of the following items. For an example of a completed IEP, see pages 134–139.

1. **A statement about your child's present levels of educational performance.** For example, if your child is in the sixth grade but reading at a second-grade level, your child's present level of educational performance in reading would be stated on the IEP as "2nd grade" or "2.0 level." Present levels of performance are usually determined by examining achievement test scores and/or class work such as written assignments and tests. They should be stated for each class in which your child needs special help or modifications.

2. **Annual goals.** Also called "long-term learning goals," these are clear statements about the educational and behavioral accomplishments your child will be expected to make by the end of the school year. Example: "To increase Tiffany's reading level from 2nd grade to 3rd grade."

3. **Short-term learning objectives with measurable goals.** Each long-term learning goal stated in the IEP should be accompanied by several short-term objectives—small steps that lead to achieving the long-term goals. For example, the long-term goal of "increasing reading level" might be broken into several short-term learning objectives, such as "add new words learned to a word bank and review twice a week," and "give five pages a week of reading in the student's special interest."

Make sure that you are involved in determining both the long-term learning goals and the short-term learning objectives. During the school year, check with the teacher often on how your child is progressing.

4. **Any special education help your child will need.** For example, you may feel that your child can learn best in a regular classroom with some special help from both the special education teacher and the classroom teacher. Perhaps you would like the regular classroom teacher to tape-record the class discussions or send home a written outline of the daily class activities so you can review these with your child each day. As a committee member, you may ask that your ideas be written into the IEP.

5. **Any other special services your child will need.** If your child will need speech therapy, transportation to and from special classes, or counseling, these services should also be written into the IEP. The law gives your child the right to receive such services if they are needed to ensure an appropriate education.

   For example, Clint is a six-year-old who has difficulty speaking. He needs to see a speech therapist every day, but he goes to a school where the speech therapist only comes twice a week. Clint's IEP includes a written statement that he will receive speech therapy every day from a therapist who works at another school a few blocks away from his own. It also includes a statement about how the school will transport Clint to the other school. If a child must go to a site away from his or her own school to receive special help, then the school district, not the parent, is responsible for providing the transportation.

6. **A statement describing how much time your child will spend in the regular classroom.** The law says that children with LD should be included in the regular classroom *to the maximum extent appropriate.* If your child will spend part of each day in the regular classroom, then the IEP should say how much time he or she will spend there. It should also say how much time your child will spend in the resource room or in the special education classroom. One goal might be for your child to spend more time in the regular classroom and less time in the special education classroom. It is your child's right to be educated with children who do not have LD, if that is where his or her educational needs are most appropriately met.

7. **Reasons why your child will not receive all of his or her education in the regular classroom, if this is the case.** If your child will spend part of the time in the special education classroom and part of the time in the regular classroom, the IEP should explain why. For example, your child may go to the special education classroom for math. The IEP should state the reason(s) why he or she can't learn math in the regular classroom.

8. **The names of all of the people who will be responsible for helping your child to reach his or her educational goals and objectives.** If your child will go to the resource room on Mondays, Wednesdays, and Fridays and spend the rest of the time in the regular classroom, the IEP should include the names of the resource room teacher and the regular classroom teacher. All of the teachers who will be working with your child should receive a copy of the IEP, because each is responsible for following the IEP requirements for his or her class.

9. **The date(s) when special education services for your child will begin, and a statement about how long they are expected to continue.**

10. **An Individualized Transition Plan (ITP).** The Individualized Transition Plan includes specific goals and objectives for preparing your child for life after high school. These might include getting a job, preparing to live independently, and taking part in school activities that build lifeskills.

    The ITP is written at the same time as the IEP. It may be a separate document, or it may be included in the IEP. IDEA states that all teenagers with LD must have a written ITP by the time they are 16 years old. We believe that it is never too soon to begin taking steps to ensure the vocational and career success of young people with LD. There's no reason why children in elementary school can't also have ITPs. If you have a younger child with LD, and if you want his or her IEP to include an ITP, then be sure to request it at the IEP meeting.

■■■■■■■■■■■■■

"Sara's IEP says that her regular classroom teacher will allow her to bring a cassette recorder to class to tape the teacher's lectures and instructions. Sara and I listen to the tape together after school. Now Sara keeps up with her work and doesn't forget important information."

Parent of a seventh grader

■■■■■■■■■■■■■

Nondiscriminatory Assessment

In the process of being referred for special education, your child will take a number of tests. Some of these tests measure aptitude, or intellectual ability; some measure academic achievement levels; some provide information about classroom behavior; and so on. Although tests can provide important information about your child, they are not perfect, and neither are the people who administer them. Tests can sometimes be used inappropriately. They may give inaccurate or irrelevant information about a particular child. To guard against situations like these, IDEA spells out the following specific rules.

1. **Tests should be given in the native language of the child who is being assessed.** Before the passage of the Education for All Handicapped Children Act of 1975 (now part of IDEA), many Spanish-speaking children were given IQ tests in English. Because they couldn't understand the questions, many of these children scored in the retarded range and were placed in special education classrooms for retarded children, where they remained until they left the public schools. Most of these children had normal or above-normal intelligence, yet they were denied access to regular classrooms.

   The law now states that a child who is tested for possible placement in special education must be tested in his or her native language, unless it is clearly not feasible to do so. Because of this mandate, IQ and achievement test questions are sometimes now translated into the child's native language.

This sometimes creates new problems, however. For a test to be truly standardized, the person administering the test must ask the questions exactly as they are written in the test manual. Translating them interferes with this standardization, making the score almost as meaningless as it would be if the child didn't understand the questions at all. For this reason, scores from translated tests may be used to draw very broad conclusions about a child's intellectual or academic performance. They should never be used as the only "proof" that a child needs special education.

2. **Tests should measure what they say they measure.** Achievement tests provide information about learning in specific school subjects—math, reading, spelling. They don't provide information about a child's intelligence or emotional condition. As a result, they should never be used to determine intelligence or the presence of emotional disorders. There are other tests designed especially for those purposes.

    Although some achievement tests will give IQ scores, these are not reliable and should never be used to make decisions about special education placement.

3. **Tests should be given by people who have been trained to give them.** No one should give your child a test that he or she has not been trained to give. This is especially important with intelligence tests, which should only be administered by a school psychologist, trained diagnostician, or psychometrician. These professionals have spent many hours learning how to give intelligence tests, and they are the *only* people who have the training necessary to interpret the scores.

    It can take several hours to complete an intelligence test. Afterward, the person who gave the test should score it and write a report about what the scores mean. The report should be written so clearly that you can read it and comprehend it. You have the right to know and understand what the test says about your child. If there's anything you don't understand, or if you need more explanation about any part of the test or score, you have the right to ask.

4. **Special education placement decisions should never be made on the basis of group intelligence test scores.** They should be based *only* on individual test scores, such as those derived from the Wechsler series of IQ tests (WPSSI, WISC-III, WAIS-R) or from the Stanford-Binet Test of Intelligence. A child's behavior can be observed during an individually administered test to determine if factors like effort, motivation, fatigue, restlessness, or illness are affecting the child's performance. On group tests, these factors cannot be taken into account.

5. **If you don't agree with the results of your child's evaluation, you may ask for an independent evaluation.** This means that you may have your child re-tested by a different person. The IEP committee must use information from the independent evaluation when they make a decision about your child's educational program. Sometimes the school will pay for an independent evaluation; sometimes you will have to pay.

6. **Scores from a single test may not be used to decide whether your child will receive special education.** Your child should never be placed in a special education program on the basis of test scores alone. Test scores should be used only as guidelines to help the IEP committee make decisions about your child's educational program. The best information should come from teachers, from yourself, and sometimes from your child.

   You should insist that your child's educational program be based on a variety of information, not just on test scores. In fact, test scores should be the *least* important factor in decisions about your child's education.

7. **Your child should be tested in all areas that might relate to his or her suspected LD.** For example, if your child is having trouble reading, he or she should not be tested only on reading ability. Other assessment information also should be considered, such as the results of an eye examination or teacher opinions about your child's reading abilities.

Maybe your child has difficulty reading because he or she had a bad experience in first grade and fell behind. In this case, a good remedial reading program might be more helpful and appropriate than special education. Or maybe your child has difficulty reading because he or she doesn't understand how letters fit together to make a word, or because the letters seem to move around on the page. In this case, your child may need to listen to tapes instead of reading books. Insist that your child be given enough tests so the specific issue can be identified and addressed.

5

Your Legal Rights as the Parent of a Child with LD

━━━━━━━━━━━━━━━━━

"If you won't advocate for your child, who will? Maybe
you'll be lucky and your child will have a special teacher. It
will help you and your child to be educated about the
school system, the services they offer, your child's learning
differences, and your legal rights as a parent. Sometimes you
may need to remind the school about your legal rights."

Parent of a fourth grader

━━━━━━━━━━━━━━━━━

Before the Education for All Handicapped Children Act was
passed in 1975, followed by IDEA in 1991, parents of children
with disabilities had no legal rights. The schools could decide
whether to include the children in their programs. They could
decide which children to place in special education and how long
to keep them there. Parents usually had no say in these decisions,
and the school didn't even have to inform parents when these decisions were made.

Things are different today. Schools must include parents in
decisions about their children's education, and most are happy to
do so. To protect and empower parents, IDEA includes three special provisions:

▶ the right to examine your child's school records,

▶ the right to an impartial due process hearing, and

▶ the right to confidentiality.

The Right to Examine Your Child's School Records

As a parent, you have the legal right to ask the school to let you
inspect any information in your child's school file. In some cases,
the school will give you a copy of your child's school records.

However, the school isn't required by law to do this unless it's impossible for you to come to the school to examine the records.

If you disagree with something that is written in your child's records, you may ask that the information be amended to reflect your opinion.

We can't emphasize strongly enough how important it is for parents to see their children's school records. Many parents never do this, either because they don't think they can or because they don't get around to it. Your child's school records might include information that will help you to understand your child better. On the other hand, they might include a comment or observation that can adversely affect the way teachers perceive your child in the future. You'll never know if you don't take the time and make the effort to find out.

~~~~~~~~~~~~~~~~~~~~~~~

"No Wonder the Child Has Problems...."

Rhoda has an adult son named Carter who has LD. Today Carter lives in Reno, has his own apartment, drives his own car, and has a full-time job. However, the school years weren't easy for Carter—or for Rhoda.

"I'll never forget a comment I found on Carter's grade school records," Rhoda says. "It was written about me when Carter was in first grade. I didn't see it until he was in high school, and I decided not to amend it because it had been written so long ago. The comment stated: 'It is no wonder the child has problems—just look at the mother!'

"At the time the comment was written, we had recently moved to a new city and enrolled Carter in the first grade at the public school. In our old city, Carter had received excellent educational services at the public school. We didn't realize that his new teacher knew *nothing* about learning differences. This was in 1971, when kids with LD were labeled 'minimal brain injured'—MBI—and before any laws existed to protect their rights.

"After three months, the teacher called me in and told me that Carter was 'incorrigible' and 'would never learn to read.' In frustration, I pulled him out of the public school and placed him in a private school for kids with LD. At my first meeting with the teacher, I was completely frazzled, experiencing a high level of stress and anxiety. Apparently the teacher thought I had gone over the edge, because after our meeting she wrote the unflattering comment in Carter's record.

"Had I known earlier that the comment was there, I would have amended it with an explanation of the circumstances. I still wonder how many of Carter's teachers through the years read the comment, doubted my emotional stability, and had a negative opinion of Carter as a result."

The Right to an Impartial Due Process Hearing

What if you don't agree with the IEP committee's decision about your child's educational program? What if you want the school to include related services, but they refuse? If you disagree with the IEP, you may ask for a special hearing before a trained and impartial hearing officer.

Once you request the hearing, the school has a certain number of days (state laws vary) to either reach an agreement with you or to set up a hearing. If the hearing officer agrees with the school, you may ask for your case to be taken to a state court. If the hearing officer agrees with you, the school has the same right to take the case to a state court.

Fortunately, parents and schools are able to reach an agreement most of the time. Very few parents—or schools—want to ask for an impartial hearing, and even fewer want to go to state court.

The Right to Confidentiality

You have the right to ask that all of your child's records, test scores, and any other information about your child and your child's educational program be kept confidential, or private. The school may not allow anyone except for you, authorized school employees, and certain other professionals to have access to your child's school records without first obtaining written permission from you.

Before asking your permission, the school must first make sure that the person who wants to see the records has a valid reason. (For example, your family counselor may want to look at your child's test scores.) The school must keep a written record of the names of all people other than school district personnel who are given access to the records.

What to Do If You Think Your Rights Have Been Violated

If you ever have reason to believe that your legal rights—or your child's—have been violated, we urge you to discuss the matter with the appropriate school personnel as soon as possible. If you are not satisfied with the results, contact the special education branch of your state's department of education. Ask them to give you the name of a special education advocate. Tell him or her your story. The advocate may be able to help you work with the school.

~~~~~~~~~~~~~~~~~~~~~~~~~~

Parents: Know Your Rights!

1. You have the right to ask that your child be placed in the educational setting that is most appropriate for your child's learning needs.

2. You have the right to ask the regular classroom teacher to make modifications for your child in lesson presentations and class assignments.

3. You have the right to be included as a member of the IEP committee, to have a say in the development of your child's special education program, and to participate in all educational decisions that are made about your child.

4. You have the right to ask that your child be educated with children who do not have learning differences.

5. You have the right to ask for an independent evaluation of your child's abilities and aptitudes if you do not agree with the results of the school district's evaluation.

6. You have the right to examine your child's school records and to ask that inappropriate or inaccurate information be amended.

7. You have the right to request an impartial due process hearing if you and the school cannot agree about your child's special education placement and/or program.

8. You have the right to ask that all of your child's records be kept confidential.

~~~~~~~~~~~~~~~~~~~~~~~~~~

6

How LD Can Affect Your Child

━━━━━━━━━━━━━━

"My daughter, Rita, has a lot of problems with other kids teasing her. Once she was in a special education classroom where the boys were giving her a hard time. The teacher had to walk out of the room for a minute, and by the time she came back, Rita was in tears."

Parent of a fourth grader

"My son was teased and called 'stupid' lots of times and only had one friend in middle school."

Parent of a high school student

━━━━━━━━━━━━━━

Imagine being at a job for eight hours a day, five days a week, where nearly everything you do is hard for you. Your supervisor constantly corrects your mistakes and tells you that if you don't improve, you'll be terminated. Your coworkers make fun of you, and when you return home from work, your spouse complains about your job performance. You have difficulty sleeping at night, you start making excuses for missing work, and you may abuse alcohol or other drugs to dull the pain you feel.

If this sounds like a nightmare, it's similar to what many students with LD experience in their daily lives. School work is hard for them. They are corrected and criticized more often than other students. Depending on how sensitive, understanding, and knowledgeable their teachers are, this correction and criticism may be positive and helpful—or not. Many students with LD are held back a grade or threatened with being held back, which is not much different from being fired from a job. They are teased by other students. Their parents pressure them to perform better in school. Failure is an everyday reality.

Just as a miserable job and home life would adversely affect you, a learning difference—and all it involves—can adversely affect your child. We believe that you want to help your child succeed in school and in life, and for this reason, we offer the following suggestions for preventing some of the difficulties associated with LD and intervening when they occur.

Of course, these difficulties are not inevitable. Not all children with LD have all of them or any of them. Many of the children we have worked with over the years are very well-adjusted and happy in their lives. Our purpose here is to make you aware of areas that may require your attention, now or in the future, so you will know what to do if the need arises.

Common Difficulties of Children with LD

"My daughter is extremely emotional. When she gets mad, she stays mad for a long time. Her feelings escalate until they are out of control."

Parent of a fourth grader

"School is really frustrating for my son. He is complaining about it a lot more this year than ever before. He says that he doesn't like school and doesn't want to go to school."

Parent of a third grader

"My daughter's self-esteem is taking a battering at school. We have her in a program to build it up, and I can only hope that eventually she'll feel better about herself."

Parent of a fifth grader

"I'm afraid that as my son grows older, the children will become even less accepting of him and tease him more about his LD and his speech impediment."

Parent of a second grader

Feelings of Being "Dumb"

Almost universally, children with learning differences come to believe that they are "dumb." This is easy to understand. When children have difficulty with school subjects, the only reason they can think of for their poor performance is a lack of intelligence. Other children may reinforce this by calling the children "stupid" or "retarded." Adults may attribute the children's difficulties to insufficient effort, but when children with LD try harder, they still have trouble learning. This only reinforces the children's feelings that they are not smart. A vicious cycle has begun—one that's very hard to break.

Behavior Issues

Children with LD frequently exhibit disruptive behaviors in the classroom, especially before they are identified and given the proper help. Again, it's not hard to figure out why this happens. The children are frustrated about the difficulties they are having in school. They feel uncomfortable in school. The teaching methods and materials may not be right for them. They may be teased by the other children. They don't understand why they are having to struggle so hard with subjects the other students grasp more easily.

Very few children have the social and language skills to express their frustration, and lacking these skills, they do the only thing they know how: act out. This can take many forms, including verbal and physical aggressiveness, noncompliance, and sullen or mischievous behavior. Some children with LD develop a truancy habit, skipping school or pretending to be sick so they can stay home.

Low Self-Esteem

Our self-esteem is strongly affected by the feedback we get from our parents, peers, and teachers. For children with LD, much of that feedback is negative. They are told that they are "not trying hard enough" or that they are "lazy." It is hard for them to make friends when the other children tease them. If inappropriate behaviors develop, the children may be labeled "troublemakers" or "bad kids."

There is a clear connection between difficulties that may arise as a result of a child's LD and the development of the child's self-esteem. We feel that this is one of the greatest barriers to giving children with learning differences the help they need. If they persist in thinking of themselves as "dumb," "lazy," and "bad"— and if these negative self-images are constantly reinforced by adults and other children—this presents a tremendous obstacle that even superb teaching and great materials may be challenged to overcome. This is one reason we advocate the early identification of students with LD. The sooner they can receive the special help they need, the less their self-esteem will suffer.

Social Difficulties

As we explained in Chapter 1, some social difficulties that children with LD experience are caused by a specific type of learning difference—social perceptual disability. Other social difficulties may result from teasing or from a child's discomfort and frustration with school.

Some children with LD withdraw from other children and become loners. Some choose younger children as friends, since younger children are less likely to be aware of the older children's academic difficulties and also because older children automatically have higher status. Many children with LD gravitate toward other students who are also having a hard time with school. This may represent security and comfort to them, since they are less likely to be rejected by children who have also been labeled "troublemakers" or "bad kids." Unfortunately, when these students form a group, they reinforce one another's inappropriate and disruptive behaviors.

Emotional Difficulties

Many children with LD develop emotional difficulties as a result of not being properly identified and/or not receiving the instruction or class placement they need. Some come from families with issues that are not being addressed.

Adolescence can be a particularly difficult time for children with LD, even if they are in good LD programs. All adolescents are very sensitive to anything that sets them apart from the other students, and having LD certainly qualifies. Children who previously seemed well-adjusted and happy may develop emotional difficulties when they reach their teens. The most common of these is depression.

It's important to know that depressed children and teens often behave differently than depressed adults. While adults may seem subdued or sad, children and teens may become irritable and angry. They also may exhibit difficulties related to sleeping and eating. Some withdraw from interacting with others, and their depression goes unnoticed.

Alcohol and Other Drug Use

Among the many reasons why people use alcohol and other drugs is to alter or cover up negative feelings. Children and teens with LD have more than their share of negative feelings. They have poor self-esteem and may feel angry and frustrated most of the time. If they have social difficulties, they may also be sad and lonely.

Like any group of young people today, those with LD have opportunities and pressures to use alcohol and other drugs. If they do experiment, they may find that these substances temporarily relieve their negative feelings. This puts them at risk of alcohol and other drug abuse and dependence. In our research, we have found that two and one-half times as many adolescents with LD as those without LD were classified as chemically dependent.

What You Can Do When Your Child Has Difficulties

"The most important lesson I've learned is this:
Accept your child for who he or she is—unique,
wonderful, filled with many gifts to share."

Parent of a twelfth grader

"Recently my son said, 'My brain doesn't work.' Sometimes I'm afraid that he won't develop sufficient coping skills to compensate for the difficulties he has with learning. When he gets frustrated, he puts his hands on his head and the pain shows on his face, and you wish you could go inside his head and fix it, but you can't. So you learn how to step back and support him without jumping in and taking over."

Parent of a third grader

Support, Encourage, and Guide

Together we have more than 40 years of experience working with children with LD and their parents. We believe that support, encouragement, and guidance from parents are the *most* important tools to use when addressing and preventing the difficulties children with LD most often have.

▶ *Support* includes helping your child understand his or her learning difference, dealing with the feelings the child has about his or her LD, and becoming a sounding-board for your child's frustrations with LD. It also includes using supportive language. You'll notice that we don't use words like "learning problem" or "problem behavior" in this book. We prefer language like "difficulty," "challenge," "concern" or "issue." Sometimes when we label something a problem, it *becomes* a problem.

▶ *Encouragement* means becoming a cheerleader for your child's efforts in academic *and* non-academic areas.

▶ *Guidance* can take many forms, such as setting up a particular time in the afternoon or evening for homework, helping your child prioritize schoolwork and home chores, pointing your child toward activities at which he or she has a good chance of succeeding, and facilitating positive friendships. All children need guidance and structure. Children with LD may need more than other children, especially when it comes to starting and completing academic tasks.

It's important to distinguish support, encouragement, and guidance from rescuing. All children make mistakes, misbehave, and deliberately do things they aren't supposed to do. Some children with learning differences may use their LD as an excuse for acting out or failing to complete assignments. All children need to learn that there are consequences for their behavior, and children with LD need to learn that they can't use LD as an excuse for inappropriate behavior. Although it's hard to see children unhappy, it's far better for them to experience the consequences of their behavior than to be rescued by well-meaning parents.

Be a Good Listener

One of the first skills counselors are taught is how to listen effectively. This means giving your full attention to the speaker and avoiding judgmental statements and premature advice and reassurance—tough to do when you're dealing with your child.

Imagine that your second-grader—let's call her Sue Ellen—comes home from school in tears because she was asked to read in front of the class and some of the other children laughed at her. Naturally, she's hurt and upset, as are you. So you say things like, "Don't worry, honey, it will be all right," or "Those children are just stupid. Don't pay any attention to them." You wipe away her tears, give her a hug and a treat, and soon Sue Ellen is quietly watching television. You are relieved that your daughter seems to be feeling better.

In fact, the situation at school may not be all right. It may continue or get worse. Sue Ellen may not be able to ignore the teasing of the other children. Furthermore, she may start to bury her feelings instead of expressing them.

To be a good listener, you need to let your child express himself or herself with minimal interruption or comments from you. When you do say something, try to paraphrase or "mirror" what your child has said. Examples: Sue Ellen says, "I almost cried when they laughed at me." You say, "That must have hurt a lot." She says, "I hate reading to the class." You say, "You feel embarrassed because reading aloud is hard for you." You're letting her know that it's okay for her to express her feelings, and that you understand how she feels.

It may seem as if this technique only prolongs the child's discomfort, but in fact, people need to express their feelings and to be understood before they can take action. After Sue Ellen has the chance to talk about her feelings and maybe even cry some more, she will be ready to discuss what to do about the reasons behind her feelings. Maybe she needs to talk to the teacher about her difficulties with reading aloud. Maybe the teacher needs to talk to the students about teasing. Together, you and Sue Ellen can explore a variety of possible solutions. Of course, this takes more time and effort than giving your child a hug and a treat, but it's worth it.

Please understand that we're not telling you *not* to reassure your child or hug your child or offer your child a treat. Instead, we're suggesting that you use effective listening *in addition to* showing your affection and support.

If you want to know more about listening skills, we recommend the following books:

▶ *How to Talk So Kids Will Listen and Listen So Kids Will Talk* by A. Faber and E. Maslish (New York: Avon Books, 1982). This book is also available on audio cassette.

▶ *P.E.T. in Action* by T. Gordon and J. Sands (New York: Bantam Doubleday Dell, 1984).

Build on Your Child's Strengths

Think about an area that you have difficulties with personally—for example, computers. For some reason, you must go to a school that emphasizes your area of weakness. You work on computers for most of each day. You always have homework related to computers, and your parents always ask you how your computer skills are progressing. It doesn't take long for you to feel completely discouraged.

This is a scenario that many children with LD live with daily, especially if their difficulties are mostly in the area of reading. Obviously reading is important, but no one wants to spend all of their time on the one area they struggle with the most. Your child probably has some area, academic or otherwise, that he or she is interested in and competent at. Encourage your child in this area and pay attention to his or her accomplishments. This is a great way to build your child's self-esteem, and his or her expertise may bring recognition at school and at home. Additionally, accomplishment in a nonacademic area, especially the arts, can motivate a child to improve his or her academic skills.

We worked with a student named Richard who was a very poor reader. But Richard loved motorcycles, and he wanted to be able to read motorcycle magazines so he could learn more about his passion. We talked with his teacher, and she agreed that some of his reading assignments could be from motorcycle magazines. This gave him the encouragement and incentive he needed to work harder on his reading in school.

Strengthen Your Child's Self-Esteem

Building on your child's strengths is an excellent way to boost his or her self-esteem. There are many books available that can give you even more ideas for helping your child. Following are some titles we know and have found useful:

▶ *Building Self-Esteem and Confidence in Yourself and Your Child* by C. Rollins (New York: Galahad Books, 1994).

▶ *100 Ways to Enhance Self-Concept in the Classroom*, 2nd edition, by J. Canfield and H. Wells (Boston: Allyn and Bacon, 1994).

▶ *Positive Self-Talk for Children: Teaching Self-Esteem through Affirmations* by D. Bloch with J. Merritt (New York: Bantam Books, 1993).

▶ *Self-Esteem: A Family Affair* by J. Clarke (San Francisco: HarperSanFrancisco, 1985).

Here are some books that can help young people build their own self-esteem:

▶ *Just Because I Am: A Child's Book of Affirmation* by L.M. Payne, M.S.W., illustrated by C. Rohling (Free Spirit Publishing, 1994).

▶ *Liking Myself* by P. Palmer (San Luis Obispo, CA: Impact Publishers, 1977).

▶ *Stick Up For Yourself! Every Kid's Guide to Personal Power and Positive Self-Esteem* by G. Kaufman and L. Raphael (Free Spirit Publishing, 1990).

▶ *Teen Esteem: A Self-Direction Manual for Young Adults* by P. Palmer and M.A. Frochner (San Luis Obispo, CA: Impact Publishers, 1989).

The more your child knows about LD, and the better your child understands his or her own learning difference, the stronger and more self-confident your child will feel. You may discover that you can share with your child some of the information you learn in this book. As you continue to find out more about LD, share that information as well. We have written three books especially for young people with LD, and you may decide that one or more of these is right for your child. They are:

▶ *The Survival Guide for Kids with LD* (Free Spirit Publishing, 1990). This book is also available on audio cassette.

▶ *The School Survival Guide for Kids with LD* (Free Spirit Publishing, 1991).

▶ *The Survival Guide for Teenagers with LD* (Free Spirit Publishing, 1993). This book is also available on audio cassette.

On pages 140–142, you'll find lists of books for and about children with learning differences. Consult the school counselor, school social worker, or school psychologist for additional suggestions appropriate to your child's age and needs. The resource room at the school might have a lending library of books for teachers and parents.

Sharpen Your Parenting Skills

We're both parents, and we know how hard it is to raise children, especially children with learning differences. If you have any concerns about your parenting skills, or if you just want to learn more about how to be an effective parent, you might want to take a parenting class or two. Check with your local parks and recreation department, YMCA/YWCA, community mental health center, school district, or place of worship. Ask other parents you know and respect to tell you about their experiences with their children and how they have learned to be better parents.

Many books have been written about parenting, and you may find some of these helpful as well. Since it's easy to get over-whelmed by the sheer numbers of titles available at your library or bookstore, you may want to begin by asking for recommendations from someone who knows you and your child—perhaps the school counselor, school social worker, or school psychologist. Here are some titles we know and recommend:

▶ *The Answer is NO: Saying It and Sticking To It* by C. Whitman, M.S.W. (Pasadena, CA: Perspective Publishing, Inc., 1994).

▶ *Grounded for Life?! Stop Blowing Your Fuse and Start Communicating with Your Teenager* by L.F. Tracy, M.S. (Seattle, WA: Parenting Press, 1994).

▶ *Raising a Daughter: Parents and the Awakening of a Healthy Woman* by J. Elium and D. Elium (Berkeley, CA: Celestial Arts, 1994). This book is also available on audio cassette.

▶ *Raising a Son: Parents and the Making of a Healthy Man* by D. Elium and J. Elium (Hillsboro, OR: Beyond Words Publishing, Inc., 1992). This book is also available on audio cassette.

▶ *Systematic Training for Effective Parenting* by G.D. McKay and D. Dinkmeyer (Circle Pines, MN: American Guidance Service, 1989).

▶ *Win the Whining War & Other Skirmishes: A Family Peace Plan* by C. Whitman, M.S.W. (Pasadena, CA: Perspective Publishing, Inc., 1991).

Teach Your Child Ways to Relax and Reduce Stress

If you feel that your child is experiencing a great deal of anxiety and stress, spend a few moments teaching your child two simple relaxation techniques:

▶ Close your eyes, take three deep breaths, and count to ten very slowly and quietly.

▶ Say "Relax" to yourself five times very slowly and quietly.

Ask your child which technique he or she prefers. Then encourage your child to use this technique anytime he or she feels frustrated, anxious, angry, or stressed.

To find out more about stress, how it affects young people, and what they can do about it, you may want to read the following books. They are written for young people, so be sure to share them with your child.

▶ *Dr. Weisinger's Anger Work-Out Book* by H. Weisinger (New York: William Morrow and Company, 1985).

▶ *Don't Pop Your Cork on Mondays: The Children's Anti-Stress Book* by A. Moser (Kansas City, MO: Landmark Editions, 1988).

▶ *Fighting Invisible Tigers: A Stress Management Guide for Teens* by E. Hipp (Free Spirit Publishing, 1995).

Get Help

Parents often feel that they have to take on all the roles that will meet their child's needs. However, there are times when a child's difficulties can best be addressed by a mental health professional. If you believe that your child needs more help than you can give, if you feel uncertain about what to do to help your child, or even if you just want a second opinion and some practical advice, don't hesitate to ask.

Most schools have some type of mental health professional—a school counselor, social worker, or psychologist—who can refer you to counseling services in your community. If your child's school doesn't have a mental health professional on staff or on call, or if you don't want to consult with the school about this particular issue, there may be a community mental health center in your area. Universities and community colleges often have counseling centers that provide referrals or counseling services for the community. Your family physician may also be a good source of information and referrals.

7

How LD Can Affect Your Family

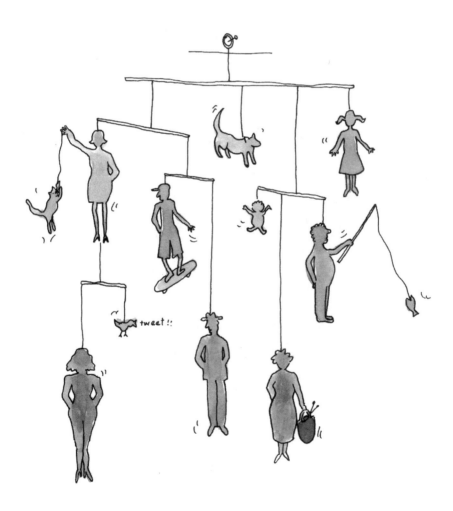

■■■■■■■■■■■■■■■■

"My daughter has LD; my son doesn't. My son often
says, 'You're always working with Angie and you never
have time for me.' But he never needs any help with his
school work. He just keeps bringing home perfect papers.
He likes the attention, so I try to spend time with him, but
he doesn't get nearly as much attention as Angie."

Parent of a third-grade daughter and fifth-grade son

■■■■■■■■■■■■■■■

Virginia Satir, the noted family therapist, once used the analogy
of a mobile to describe a family. Each section of the mobile is separate from every other section, but is also connected to at least one
other section by a string or wire. If one section of the mobile is
moved, every other section reacts to the movement until the
mobile again comes to rest.

In families, if an event occurs which disrupts the normal func-
tioning of one family member, each person in the family reacts to
it. For example, let's imagine a traditional family of four: Mom,
Dad, and two children, a boy age two and a girl age six. Mom gets
the flu and stays in bed for two to three days. This event shakes up
the family and results in each family member having to make a
personal adjustment. If Mom typically cooks for the family, Dad
must take over this role and also care for his children and his wife.
The two-year-old may not understand illness and will wonder why
Mom won't play with him. The six-year-old may be asked to be a
"big girl" and to take on some adult roles, such as caring for her
younger brother or getting things for her mother.

Families handle minor disruptions in different ways, depending
on the flexibility of roles within the family, the family's method of
solving problems, family communication patterns, and child management techniques. For example, if the father in one family is
used to performing household chores and being involved in the

care of his children, the mother's illness may be less disruptive than if he has not been involved in these activities.

When a family determines that a child has learning differences, a major disruption occurs in the family mobile, and each family member must react and adjust to this event.

The Harrison Family

The Harrison family consists of Sara, the mother; ten-year-old-Reggie; and three-year-old Denise. Sara and the children's father, Fred, are divorced, but Fred still takes an active interest in his children and sees them regularly. Fred is an auto mechanic and Sara is the accountant for a discount department store.

Reggie was identified as having LD at the age of seven. Although Fred was never identified as LD, he was a very poor reader and didn't complete high school. When Sara told Fred that Reggie needed special education assistance, Fred became very angry, insisting that Reggie was "no dummy" and shouldn't have to go to "a class for retards." Sara asked the school to hold Reggie back a year instead, and he repeated the first grade. When he continued to struggle, Sara and Fred finally agreed to special education placement.

Reggie began to act out in school, frequently fighting with other students and swearing at teachers. Periodically Fred would call the school and demand that Reggie be taken out of the "retard" classes. Sara would usually attend school conferences, but she usually had little to say. She often brought Denise with her to the conferences; the child was always quiet and withdrawn, and would sit and suck her thumb while holding her blanket.

Fred reacted to Reggie's LD with frustration and anger, most likely because of his own difficult experiences while he was in school. Both Sara and Denise reacted by withdrawing.

The Stewart Family

The Stewart family consists of two parents, Bob and Maggie; fourteen-year-old Shelly; nine-year-old Harry; and eight-year-old Jerome. Bob is an orthopedist and Maggie works in the home. Shelly and Harry are good students. Jerome, however, was born prematurely and had health problems as an infant. Although his health improved over time, his language development was slow, and in first grade he was identified as having LD.

Maggie took Jerome to a number of different medical centers and visited a variety of psychologists, speech therapists, and other professionals for testing and treatment. She read everything she could find about LD and became very familiar with special education. She regularly visited Jerome's resource room at school and was actively involved in the development of his IEP. She told the resource room teacher that she wondered if her age (40) at the time of Jerome's birth might have been the cause of her son's learning difficulties.

When Bob found out that his son had LD, he distanced himself from Jerome and the rest of his family. He told Maggie that he thought LD was "baloney" and that Jerome's biggest problem was that Maggie "babied him too much." He began to spend longer hours at work.

Meanwhile, Shelly continued to excel in school and began to involve herself in more school activities. Harry's school performance began to deteriorate, and he started getting into trouble at school and around the neighborhood.

Each member of the Stewart family reacted to Jerome's LD in a different way. Because of her guilt, Maggie became overly involved in Jerome and his difficulties, neglecting herself and the rest of her family. Bob avoided the issue through denial and blame. Shelly tried to refocus attention on herself through high achievement, and Harry tried to do the same through misbehaving.

Coping with the Loss of a Dream

"I've tried not to be too hard on-myself, but ever
since I learned that my son has LD, I've lost my self-
confidence. I keep wondering what I could have
done for things to turn out differently."

Parent of a second grader

Both the Harrisons and the Stewarts reacted to having a child
with LD in typical but nonproductive ways. Most parents hope that
their children will have the necessary attributes and abilities to lead
successful lives, and most want their children to achieve even more
than they have.

When a child is born who does not fulfill the parents' hopes,
whether because of a physical or mental disability or a learning difference, the parents' dream dies, and they experience a profound
sense of loss at the death of their dream. They react to their loss
with denial, fear, guilt, and anger. These reactions are normal and
natural, but it is important to see beyond them and dream again,
even if the dream is not the same as before. The families that succeed are those who are able to work through their feelings and
readjust their family mobile.

Ways to Readjust Your Family Mobile

"We provide our daughter with a home where she can feel
comfortable being who she is."

Parent of a fourth grader

"My husband is my best friend. He and I talk about
our son a lot. We try to go out to dinner together every
week or two, and we sit at the table for three or four hours
just talking. That's probably my most important outlet for
my feelings of sadness and disappointment."

Parent of a first grader

1. **If you have feelings of denial, guilt, fear, and anger because of your child's LD, remember that these feelings are normal and natural.** However, if you are finding it difficult to work through these feelings, you may want to consult a family counselor. The school counselor or school psychologist should be able to refer you to a family counselor. Or check with your community health center or family doctor.

2. **Be open and honest about your child's LD.** Healthy conversation and communication among family members is usually the best way to avoid nonproductive responses to family stress. Don't treat your child's LD as a family secret. Make sure that each member of the family understands what a learning difference is.

3. **Remember that other family members still need loving attention—including your partner, any other children, and yourself.** Guilt about a child's learning differences can sometimes cause parents to become so involved with that child that they neglect everyone else in the family. While your child with LD certainly needs your support, encouragement, guidance, and attention, so do your other family members. Try to balance the amount of time you spend with each of your children, and make sure to leave ample time for your partner and yourself.

4. **Realize that you can't protect your child from being hurt or feeling sad.** Although it's painful to know that your child will sometimes feel frustrated, angry, hurt, and sad, and it's hard to realize that your child will probably have to endure teasing and cruelty from other children, you can't protect your child from

the world. What you can do is listen, be supportive, and help your child to develop appropriate coping skills.

Work together on a list of things your child can do when he or she feels frustrated, angry, hurt, or sad. Encourage your child to talk about the feelings, and be a good listener. Then do something together that you both enjoy. How about taking a walk, playing a game, reading a story, or baking cookies? Ask your child for ideas.

Practice with your child various ways to cope with teasing. Following are four suggestions that we often share with the children we work with:

▶ Stand up straight and look the other person in the eye. In a calm voice, say, "I don't like to be talked to in that way." Then walk away.

▶ Talk to an adult you like and trust. Choose someone who cares about you and who is a good listener. Tell that person about the teasing and how it makes you feel.

▶ Don't tease other people. You're less likely to be teased if you don't tease.

▶ Remember that you can't control the people who tease you. You can't make them stop teasing. But you can control what you do when they tease you. You can choose to stand up to the teaser, speak up for yourself, and feel good about yourself.

5. **Keep yourself physically, mentally, emotionally, and spiritually healthy.** If you're immobilized by guilt and anger, your child will be immobilized, too. If you use alcohol or other drugs to deal with your feelings, you will be inaccessible to your child and the rest of your family. Parenting any child is a challenge; parenting a child with LD can be especially difficult. Make it easier by staying as healthy and happy as you can.

6. **Focus on the good things about your child and your life.** Your child is much more than a person with LD. Your child is a unique, complex, interesting individual—someone you love deeply. Raising a child with LD can be difficult, but it also has its rewards. Each small success is a big achievement. If your

child's learning differences result in your spending more time together, this can create a special closeness. If you talk openly about your child's LD within your family, you may find that communication improves in other areas as well. There are many positive aspects to parenting a child with LD. Be open to them and celebrate them.

The Martinez Family

There are four people in the Martinez family: Thelma, the mother; Ben, the father; eleven-year-old Rick; and nine-year-old Kimberly.

Thelma is an educator, and Ben is in retail sales. Kimberly was born prematurely and had seizures as an infant. She has been in special education since she was six and has been diagnosed as having attention deficit hyperactive disorder (ADHD) and LD. Rick is an excellent student and very popular with the other kids.

The Martinez family has had its share of frustrations, both with Kimberly and with the various professionals who have worked with her. Both Thelma and Ben attend IEP and other school meetings, where they talk assertively with school personnel about Kimberly's special education placement and her goals and objectives. They usually manage to remain calm during the meetings, but they also have agreed on a "signal" to send so one parent knows when the other is feeling too emotional to talk.

With both parents employed outside of the home, it's hard to find time for their kids and each other. But Thelma and Ben have worked out a plan so that each parent spends at least half an hour with each child every night. At least once a month, they get a sitter and go out to dinner and a movie by themselves. Thelma and Ben both say that there is plenty of conflict and disruption in their lives, but they feel supported by each other and appreciate the uniquenesses of each of their children.

8

~~~~~~~~~~~~~~~~~

Coping with Curious Friends, "Helpful" Relatives, and Nosy Strangers

Many people—including professionals—don't understand what it means to have a learning difference. Like other conditions that people have "read something about" or "heard something about," your child's LD may inspire a lot of annoying questions and unsolicited suggestions. Strangers or acquaintances may ask, "What's wrong with your child?" Friends and family members may offer to share "treatments" they have discovered or researched for you.

However well-intentioned other people may be, their inquiries and advice can get irritating. And when you are repeatedly asked what you did to "cause" your child's LD, it's understandable that you will feel defensive or guilty. You may wonder if you're doing everything you can to help your child, especially when well-meaning relatives tell you about "cures" they saw on television.

We don't know of a "cure" for LD. We also don't know of a "cure" for rudeness or unsolicited advice. But we do have some suggestions for ways you might respond. Of course, you can always say "I'd rather not discuss it" when you don't want to answer a question, or "Thank you" when someone offers advice.

Dealing with Questions

Q: **What is a "learning disability"?**

A: We call it a "learning difference." It means that our son's way of learning reading (spelling, arithmetic) is different than most other children's.

Q: **I don't understand what you mean by "learning difference." Can you explain?**

A: Let me ask you a question: If you wanted to learn how to build a table, how would you do it? Would you take a class? Watch a video? Read a book? Or would you buy some wood and just start building? We all learn differently. For kids with LD, this becomes really obvious in school, because they don't learn well in traditional ways.

Q: Is your child slow (stupid, retarded)?

A: It's hard for her to learn some things. But she's not stupid, and she's definitely not retarded! Most kids with learning differences have average or above average intelligence, and some are gifted. They learn many things just as well as or better than other children.

Q: Does he have dyslexia?

(NOTE: If your child has difficulty with reading, you can use this response. If not, just say "no.")

A: Dyslexia is a kind of learning difference in which someone has a lot of trouble with reading. Many children with learning differences have difficulties learning to read, but they don't have dyslexia. Also, the word "dyslexia" is a term we don't like to use. It implies that there is something wrong with our child, and there is nothing wrong with our child.

Q: I've heard that children with LD see letters and words upside down. Is that true?

A: Very few children with learning differences actually see letters and words incorrectly. Many children, even those who don't have LD, confuse letters like "b" and "d" and words like "saw" and "was" when they are learning to read. Children with LD who are learning to read can take longer than other children to learn the difference between words and letters that look the same.

Q: How did your child get this way?

A: Nobody really knows what causes LD. But everybody has some kind of learning difference. We all have things we learn easily, and things we learn slowly.

Q: Did you take some kind of drug when you were pregnant? Is that why your child is LD?

A: No, and no.

Q: Is there a cure for LD?

A: LD isn't a disease. If someone has trouble learning to play the trumpet, we don't talk about "curing her music LD." We make sure that she has the right teacher, the right instrument, and the right materials. We give her a lot of support and encouragement and time to practice. Eventually she'll learn to play the trumpet. And eventually, many children with LD can learn academic skills if they receive the appropriate educational opportunities.

Some questions may be unbelievably rude and hurtful. We're still amazed at the things people ask each other. When faced with a question that leaves you speechless, just walk away. Or try this all-purpose response: "Why do you want to know?"

Dealing with Advice

Here's our best advice about advice: Unless you're personally familiar with current research in the field of learning differences, it's hard to dispute the findings of so-called "experts" who may be quoted in newspapers or magazines or invited to comment on talk shows. Instead of arguing with someone who tells you what you should do with, for, or about your child, try saying something like this:

"We appreciate the information. But we work very hard to make sure that Bobby doesn't feel there is something 'wrong' with him. Children with LD are very aware that they don't learn some things as quickly as other kids do. We try to get Bobby the best possible instruction in school. We support and encourage his efforts in the areas he has trouble in, and we help him to focus on the areas he does well in. That's how we have chosen to help our son. We hope you'll support our way of helping Bobby."

9

Do's and Don'ts
for Helping Your Child

> "The best way I've been able to help my son is
> by letting go of my ideas of what's 'normal.'
> I just accept him the way he is."
>
> *Parent of a sixth grader*

For many parents who learn that their child has LD, their first response is to ask, "What can we do to help our child overcome this?" They may search frantically for professional help, spending months or years looking for a "cure" for their child's learning difference. We are amazed at the sheer resiliency of children who have endured vitamin treatments, dietary restrictions, bizarre physical exercises, after-school tutors, summer school programs, play therapy, psychologists, counselors, speech therapists, eye exercises, and more. Rhoda has had personal experience at this; she subjected her son, Carter, to most of these treatments and spend a small fortune in the process.

While some of these approaches may help some children, none of them will "cure" LD. With or without these methods, most children with LD can learn to compensate for their learning differences, and many will grow up to be happy, successful, competent adults. What seems to do the most good? Not vitamins, not exercises, not even special programs or advice from experts. These children succeed primarily because of their parents' love, encouragement, and support.

We don't mean to discourage you from seeking help for your child, if that's what you decide to do. In Chapter 11, we'll even offer some suggestions you may want to try. Meanwhile, we *do* mean to encourage you to relax (at least some of the time), take care of yourself, and enjoy the remarkable, interesting, intelligent, complex person your child already is.

The following do's—and don'ts—can help you to have a positive, healthy relationship with your child, the kind of relationship that is good for both of you. All of these suggestions are based on our personal experiences working with children with LD and their parents. Many come from Rhoda's life with her son, Carter.

DO Love Your Child and Show It

"I try to help my son deal with the frustrations
of his relationships with peers, adults, and teachers,
and to cope with what they expect from him.
I try to keep his self-esteem high."

Parent of a seventh grader

We believe that a parent's love is the strongest force in a child's life. Children with LD get bumped and banged around a lot as they move through the school years. However, most of them can withstand just about anything when they know that their parents love and support them.

Think of as many ways as you can to show your love to your children. Spend time with them, tell them you love them over and over, hold them, hug them, kiss them, be happy for them, be happy with them, snuggle them, hold their hand, touch their hair, cry over them, stick up for them, encourage them, support them, learn what they like best and share it with them. There are countless ways to say "I love you!" How many can you think of? For ideas, you might want to read these books:

▶ *101 Ways to Tell Your Child "I Love You"* by V. Lansky (Chicago: Contemporary Books, Inc., 1988).

▶ *101 Ways to Make Your Child Feel Special* by V. Lansky (Chicago: Contemporary Books, Inc., 1991).

▶ *Love* by L. Buscaglia (New York: Fawcett, 1993).

DO Let Go and Stand Back with Your Arms Open

Give your child as many opportunities as possible to learn the meaning of independence and freedom: independence to think, act, and react; freedom to do, be, and hope. Allow your child enough independence to make mistakes and enough freedom to fall. But always stand behind your child and keep your arms open in case you need to break the fall. Too much independence, too soon, can frighten a child; too much freedom, too soon, can make a child feel abandoned and insecure.

To grow, all children need the opportunity to make mistakes and learn not to make the same mistakes again. We believe that children with LD also should be allowed to learn from their mistakes. As a parent, you should protect your child from real danger, but you should not *overprotect* your child to such an extent that he or she never has the chance to learn the coping skills needed to avoid repeating mistakes.

DO Spend Time with Your Child

Most of us are so busy these days that we scarcely have enough time and energy to do our jobs and complete our chores, much less spend time with our family. Children with LD can take up a lot of their parents' time, most of which is spent on dealing with school issues and concerns. While it's necessary to spend *some* time on school-related matters, it's equally important to relax with your child, whether you're reading, playing, talking, or just sitting quietly together. Please don't let yourself become so consumed with your child's learning difference that you forget to spend time enjoying each other.

DO Respond Appropriately to Inappropriate Behaviors

Sometimes parents feel sorry for their children with LD. They feel so sorry for them that they fail to respond appropriately when their children misbehave. Like any other kids, children with learning differences can be opportunistic. They may have trouble with school subjects, but they quickly figure out how to take advantage of their parents!

Children with LD need structure and discipline as much as, if not more than, other children. As they grow up, they will meet plenty of adults who pity them because of their LD and let them get away with inappropriate behaviors. To counter these misguided attempts to "help" their children, parents must present a united front at home and never hesitate to respond when a child misbehaves.

Piaget believed that children expect one of two kinds of "punishment," depending on their developmental stage: *expiatory punishment* or *punishment by reciprocity.* Expiatory punishment is handed down by authoritative adults when a child breaks the rules. It is firm but never abusive, and it doesn't have to "fit the crime." It is most effective until children reach the age of nine or ten.

If you are the parent of a younger child, it's perfectly acceptable for you to use your authority as a parent to say, "You took your sister's toy. Go to your room now, because I said so!" Young children expect their parents to exert such authority, and they respect them for doing so.

Once children reach age nine or ten and begin to express their need for autonomy and independence, expiatory punishment ceases to work. At this age, the most effective response is punishment by reciprocity, where the punishment does fit the crime.

Today we are more likely to call this "the use of logical consequences." Rather than handing down rules, which older children are likely to rebel against, parents work with their children to establish mutually agreed upon consequences for specific actions. Example: "You left your dirty plate and half-filled milk glass next to the TV. You know you're supposed to clean up after yourself when you eat in the living room—those are the terms for being allowed to eat there. Because you didn't clean up after yourself, eating in the living room is off limits for the rest of the week." Or: "You came home an hour past curfew last night. We agreed that if this ever happened, you would come home an hour earlier than curfew the next time you went out with your friends. When you go out next Friday night, we'll expect you home by 8:00."

Does "grounding" work? Not for most children and adolescents, since it seldom fits the crime. However, grounding can sometimes force a young person to slow down and take stock of his or her behavior, and that can be a benefit.

Regardless of your child's age, we encourage you to respond *appropriately* to inappropriate behaviors. This is not a concept that many parents understood when we were children (how many of us felt that the punishment fit the crime?), so if you need more information about it, you may want to read the following books:

▶ *Children: The Challenge* by R. Dreikurs, M.D., and L. Zuckerman (New York: NAL-Dutton, 1991).

▶ *Discipline without Tears: What to Do with Children Who Misbehave* by R. Dreikurs, M.D. and P. Cassel (New York: NAL-Dutton, 1990).

▶ *Logical Consequences: The New Approach to Discipline* by R. Dreikurs (New York: NAL-Dutton, 1994).

▶ *Time Out: A Guide for Parents and Teachers Using Popular Discipline Methods to Empower and Encourage Children* by J. Nelson and H.S. Glenn (Fair Oaks, CA: Sunrise Press, 1992).

Whatever logical consequences you use, make sure to separate the child from the behavior. Example: "Throwing rocks at windows is not a good way to act. You'll have to use your allowance for the next few weeks to pay for the windows you broke." This separates the child from the inappropriate behavior. This, however, does not: "You're always wrecking things. I can't believe you broke another window. You're so clumsy that you can forget about your allowance for the next few weeks." In the first example, the child is told, "What you did was wrong, and you need to make it right." In the second example, the child is told, "YOU are wrong." Which would you rather hear?

DO Allow Your Child To Have Many and Varied Experiences

"I help my daughter to focus on her strengths,
and I encourage her to pursue her areas of interest.
We try to expose her to all sorts of experiences."

Parent of an eighth grader

Many children with LD do not pick up information incidentally. In other words, they don't always learn just by observation or by living. This is especially true when it comes to social behaviors. Often, children with LD lack friends because they lack the interpersonal skills necessary to be a friend.

We believe that social learning is just as important—perhaps more important—than academic learning. But social skills are not always taught in school, and it becomes the parents' responsibility to teach their children how to make and keep friends. The best way to do this is by giving children plenty of opportunities to interact with others in social settings.

Some children with LD are overly active. They tend to behave inappropriately in social situations—laughing too loud, running around too much, getting too physical with the other children. It may be stressful for you to watch your child try to make friends and sometimes fail. Don't give up! Let your child know when he or she is acting inappropriately. Give concrete explanations. Example: "Tracy cried because you yelled at her and hurt her feelings." This is much more helpful than "Stop yelling at Tracy!"

On pages 90–91, you'll find several suggestions for making and keeping friends to share with your child. Talk about each one. See if your child can think of ideas to try. Be positive and encouraging.

Tips for Making and Keeping Friends

☞ Keep your eyes and ears open. Watch and listen during lunch, before and after school, in your neighborhood, at your community center. Is there someone else who seems to need a friend? Do you see a group of kids who get along without teasing or fighting? Is someone involved in an activity that seems interesting to you? These are all good possibilities for friends.

☞ Get involved in games where people line up to play and take turns.

☞ Don't try to *make* other people be your friends. Nobody can force another person to like them.

☞ Become an expert. Learn as much as you can about music, cars, baseball cards, movies, or anything else kids your age are interested in. When you hear other students talk about it, join in. You'll have something to contribute, and you'll feel more confident about taking part in the conversation. (Just don't act as if you know *everything* about the subject. Be willing to listen and learn.)

☞ Don't try to "buy" friends with gifts or favors. Real friends don't take advantage of each other. They give and take. There should be times when you do favors for your friends, and times when they do favors for you.

☞ Join a group or a club. Find one that matches one of your interests. Many groups welcome new members. Look around your school, church or temple, or community for possibilities.

☞ Make the first move. Don't just stand around waiting for people to come to you. Start a conversation with someone. This can be scary—what if the person tells you to get lost or makes fun of you? On the other hand, he or she may want to be friends, too. You'll never know unless you try.

- ☞ Don't look for friends only among the most popular kids. You might find good friends in students who aren't part of the "in crowd."

- ☞ When you play with others, be polite, take your turn, and be a good sport. Give compliments when people deserve them. Examples: "Nice shot!" "Good save!" "Great job!"

- ☞ Be a good listener. If most of your sentences start with "I," you need to practice listening.

- ☞ Don't wander around by yourself, hoping someone will ask you to join them. Instead, ask someone to join you, perhaps to play a game or shoot hoops or take a walk.

- ☞ Choose your friends carefully. Stay away from kids who are always in trouble or acting out.

- ☞ Most people like to talk about themselves. Try asking other people questions about what they like to do. Or ask them about their favorite TV shows, sports, music, or games. Find out what they like, and they might ask you what *you* like, and suddenly you'll find yourself in a friendly conversation.

- ☞ Don't show off or get into trouble to get noticed.

- ☞ Leave some space. When you make a new friend, it's easy to go too far. You want to spend all of your time with him or her. This is a good way to *lose* friends. Leave some space in your friendship for other people and for yourself. Don't be jealous of the time your friend spends with other people.

- ☞ Treat other people the way you want to be treated.

- ☞ Ask for help. If you're having trouble making friends, talk to an adult you like and trust—a parent, a teacher you respect, a school counselor, your minister or rabbi.

- ☞ Like yourself. Value and respect yourself. Let it show—by keeping yourself neat and clean, being true to yourself and your beliefs, staying healthy, and being trustworthy and responsible. Don't put yourself down. People like people who have positive self-esteem.

DO Advocate for Your Child

No one cares as much as you do about your child's well-being and success. No one knows your child as well as you do. That's why it's up to you to step in, speak up, and advocate for your child when the need arises.

Many parents of children with LD are concerned that their children aren't getting the help they need at school, but they hesitate to say anything because they're afraid of being labeled "obnoxious" or "troublemakers." Chapters 4 and 5 of this book spell out your children's rights and your rights under the law. If you feel that these rights are being ignored or abused, you have a responsibility to voice your concerns to the teacher. In most cases, the teacher will be more than happy to listen to you and work with you to resolve the issue.

Sometimes a teacher may be as concerned as you are about your child's educational program, yet be powerless to do anything because of time constraints or because of lack of support from other school personnel. As a parent, you have more clout with the administration than teachers do, plus the law is on your side. If you're worried about your child's educational program, speak up. You may be surprised at the power you have and at the difference you can make.

DO Learn as Much as You Can about Your Child's LD

Learn everything you can about learning differences in general, and about your child's specific LD in particular. Read books and articles, take a class, join a group of parents who have kids with LD. The more you know about learning differences, the more confidence you will have in your own abilities to advocate for your child.

Following are two books we know and recommend:

▶ *Parenting the Learning Disabled: A Realistic Approach* by R. Cummings and C. Maddux (Springfield, IL: Charles C. Thomas, 1985).

▶ *No Easy Answers: The Learning Disabled Child* by S.L. Smith (New York: Bantam Books, 1981).

DO Be Patient with Yourself

"Every now and then I blow it. Everyone thinks that I have it together so well all of the time, but sometimes I'm a horrible parent at home, ranting and raving and screaming and yelling. Sometimes that just happens."

Parent of a fourth grader

It's hard to be the parent of a child who has a learning difference. More than most other children, kids with LD are distractible, overactive, and sometimes just plain frustrating. They demand much from their parents and often seem to give little in return.

Most parents want to be patient and understanding with their children. But we all lose control sometimes, saying and doing things we don't mean and feel sorry for later. Surprise! Parents are human, too. We get tired, fed up, and angry—like our kids.

Obviously, you don't want to lose your temper every time your child does something that disappoints or upsets you. But we believe that an occasional outburst is normal and can even be emotionally healthy. Children need to know that their parents have feelings, too. This gives them permission to let their own feelings show.

If you believe that you get angry or lose control too often, please talk to someone about it. Check with the school counselor, school psychologist, your community health center, or your family doctor about a referral to a family counselor. It will help to talk about your frustrations, and a good counselor can give you suggestions for coping with them in positive, healthy ways.

DO Take Care of Yourself

We believe that all parents, especially parents of children with LD, should give themselves a break once in awhile. Having a child with a learning difference can be hard on you and on the other members of your family.

When things get crazy, give yourself a "time out." Here are some suggestions that have worked for us. You may want to compile your own list of "time out" ideas and keep it handy.

- Lock yourself in the bathroom with a book, a cup of hot tea, and a tubful of bubbly water. Stay there until you feel relaxed or you turn into a prune, whichever comes first.

- Escape to your car with a handful of tapes of your favorite soothing music. Drive to a park, sit back, listen to the music, and relax. If you can't leave your children alone for that long, just sit in the driveway and escape for a few moments.

- Get a sitter and go to dinner with your spouse or a friend.

- If possible, spend a few days at the beach, in the mountains, at a cabin by a lake, or at an in-town hotel.

We know that sitters and vacations are expensive; we also know that two or three days away from the children can sometimes be as refreshing as a two-week vacation. Do your best to get away once in a while. Your whole family will benefit.

DON'T Give Up

Rhoda remembers many times when Carter was a child that she felt like crawling into bed, pulling the covers over her head, and never coming out. You may feel the same on days when you're discouraged about your child's progress or simply exhausted from the never-ending challenge of parenting a child with LD.

Whatever happens, don't give up! Even when things appear to be hopeless. Even when you feel like you're at the end of your rope. Even when you think you've tried everything and nothing seems to work.

The good news is: *Most children with learning differences get better as they get older, especially once they are out of school.* We know this from our own observations and from recent research on adults with learning differences.

One researcher who studied adults with LD found that many were employed in a wide range of occupations, and only a few held unskilled jobs. Other studies describe strategies that adults with LD use to compensate for their learning differences and become more successful. The most commonly used strategies include spending extra time to complete work, asking for additional help, and carefully checking for errors. Other creative ways adults with LD compensate including having their spouses help them write reports and asking friends to assist them with spelling.

We have an adult friend with LD who can't read at all, yet he works as a letter carrier for the postal service. He asks his friends at work to help him read new addresses, and if there is a change in his route, he asks a friend to drive the route with him during his off-hours so he can memorize landmarks along the way.

Many young people with LD improve significantly after they graduate and become involved in experiences that don't demand formal academic learning. Others go on to post-secondary schooling where they can register as students with LD and receive support and modification for tests, note-taking, reading, and more. Whatever your child decides to do, he or she won't be in school forever, even if it seems that way today.

DON'T Try To Be Your Child's Teacher

"I tried to help him with his schoolwork, but I would lose my patience. We'd end up screaming at each other, or I'd be screaming and he'd be crying. One day I realized that we were spending all of our time together doing homework. I said, 'Enough is enough!' I still help him sometimes, but we also spend time together just having fun."

Parent of a third grader

Many children with LD work hard in school all day long. Then they come home to face a parent who immediately wants to sit down with them and help them with their homework. These children spend most of their waking hours working on academics.

We believe that children's time at home should be spent on more relaxing activities. What if you had to work at a frustrating job for eight long hours, then bring home another four or five hours of work to do while someone watched over you to make sure you did it? You'd probably quit your job and look for one that was less harmful to your physical and emotional well-being. Is it any wonder that many young people with LD are at risk and drop out of school as soon as they can?

Your home should be a haven for your child—a place where your child can rest, play, enjoy being with you, and enjoy being himself or herself. It should not be a night school where parents are the teachers. Some parents can successfully help their children with homework on occasion. If you are one of them, keep up the good work. However, if you find that trying to help your child is causing a lot of stress and tension between you, consider one or more of the following alternatives:

▶ Help your child *only* when he or she specifically asks for your help.

▶ See if your child's teacher can modify the homework assignments.

▶ Hire a tutor to work with your child in those subjects that present the most difficulty.

Your child already has a teacher at school. He or she needs a *parent* at home.

MaryBeth and Janna

MaryBeth is a single parent whose daughter, Janna, has LD. When Janna was in elementary school, she occasionally had homework, but most of it was fairly easy and usually took no longer than half an hour to complete.

The summer between the end of sixth grade and the beginning of seventh grade, MaryBeth made a point to visit each of Janna's five new teachers. MaryBeth was concerned that Janna might have trouble making the transition between elementary school and middle school. She wanted to be sure that the teachers knew about Janna's learning difference and her many strengths as a student and as a person.

Two weeks after Janna started seventh grade, she brought home notes from two of her teachers, both of whom described her as "lazy" and "a daydreamer." The teachers also mentioned that Janna was not doing her homework.

MaryBeth was frustrated. She had thought the teachers would be more understanding. She was also worried for her daughter. Only two weeks of school had passed, and Janna was already falling behind! MaryBeth started meeting Janna at the door each afternoon when she returned home from school. She demanded that they sit down together immediately and work on Janna's homework.

For most classes, the homework was minimal, and Janna could usually complete it within an hour. Math was another story. Each day, the math teacher assigned between 40 and 50 problems for homework. Math was Janna's weakest area, so she and MaryBeth worked together each night until 10 or 11 p.m. to finish the assignment. If Janna didn't understand how to work a particular kind of problem, MaryBeth explained it slowly and patiently. After Janna understood, she usually would work the first few problems correctly, although it took her a long time to complete each problem. To finish all 40 or 50 was extremely difficult for her, and Janna eventually would become tired and lose her grasp of how to work the problems. Then she would write down random answers—anything to get the assignment done. When Janna began making errors, or if she couldn't finish her homework by bedtime, MaryBeth took over and worked the remaining problems for her.

After a month of late nights spent doing Janna's homework, both mother and daughter hated to sit down together. Finally, their patience was exhausted. An argument escalated into a screaming fight. Janna ran to her room and slammed the door; MaryBeth wadded up the homework papers, threw them on the floor, and resolved never again to put herself or her daughter through such pain.

The next day, MaryBeth called the math teacher and explained the situation. She asked the teacher if he would modify the math assignment to include fewer problems. After all, if Janna could work 10 or 15 problems correctly, this should be sufficient to prove that she understood the concept. The math teacher agreed to make the modification MaryBeth requested.

From that point on, Janna's homework was Janna's responsibility. MaryBeth told her that it wasn't worth ruining their relationship or sacrificing their sanity. She expected Janna to do her best, and whatever happened would be fine with her.

Janna is now 17, and MaryBeth still doesn't help her with her homework unless she asks. Even then, if MaryBeth perceives the tension rising between them, she withdraws.

DON'T Overemphasize Schoolwork

Your child is so much more than the sum of his or her parts—even the learning different part. It's important to encourage your child to do well in school, but it's even more important to help your child develop into a caring, loving, likable person.

Children with LD learn many things in school that have nothing to do with their worth as individuals. As parents, it's our job to help our children feel worthwhile and valuable in spite of their learning differences. If your child brings home a bad report card, the sky won't fall. A note from the teacher about a poor test score isn't the end of the world. Try to put schoolwork into perspective: It matters, but it doesn't define your child. In response to a low test score, you might say, "I see that you didn't do so well on your math test. I know you studied, and I know you tried your hardest. You may be having trouble with math this year, but you did a great job of helping me paint the dining room last weekend. I was proud of you then, and I'm proud of you now."

DON'T Overprotect Your Child

Most parents want to protect their children from bad experiences and hurtful situations. This is perfectly normal. However, many parents of children with disabilities go too far. They are so overprotective that their children grow up to be dependent adults who can't take care of their most basic needs.

In *The Disabled and Their Parents,* Dr. Leo Buscaglia offers this perspective on a common occurrence:

"A child begins to feel the need for some separation from others as early as the first year of life. If this opportunity for separation and independence is afforded, a sense of emergent personal identity will result. It is this sensed identity to which the family must become attuned, for upon this will depend the child's future emotional and intellectual well-being and independence. This self-identity will be, eventually, responsible for his trusting his own experience, asking his own questions, deciding upon his own limitations and forming his own concept and perceptions of the world. The family's role becomes one of encouraging the child's emerging individuality and permitting him to make his own choices, to exert and express himself. In order to do this, they will have to rid themselves of their preconceived notions of his dependence, limited abilities, and inferior family status and allow him to reveal his own needs and abilities." *The Disabled and Their Parents: A Counseling Challenge* (Thorofare, NJ: Charles B. Slack, Inc., 1975).

Is your child experiencing some of the normal bumps and bruises of life? Are you giving your child the opportunity to make mistakes and learn from them? When you envision the future, do you see your child as being autonomous and independent? Do you trust your child to make decisions and choices? If you can't answer "yes" to these questions, it's possible that you're being overprotective. Back off a little and see what happens. You may be surprised at how capable your child really is.

DON'T Overindulge Your Child

Children with LD are fully as capable of being spoiled as other kids. Yet parents sometimes feel sorry for their "special" children and grant them privileges they would never extend to other children.

Alfred Adler (1870–1937) was a renowned Viennese psychologist and psychiatrist. He warned parents about the dangers of pampering their children, stressing that spoiled and overprotected children had the potential for becoming the most dangerous class in society because they would not develop social feelings and instead would become dictators who expected society to conform to their self-centered wishes.

Adler's views may seem extreme, but they define one possible cause of a result we all see far too often: children who are selfish, inconsiderate, and unaware of the needs of others. Your child will thrive on your support, encouragement, and guidance. Your child doesn't need (or deserve) extra privileges just because he or she happens to have LD.

DON'T Sacrifice Yourself

It's true that your learning different child may need more of your time and attention than your other children. But don't get so wrapped up in caring for that child that you neglect your own needs and those of your family. The happier you are, the happier they will be. You don't have to sacrifice yourself to be a capable, caring parent.

10

Ways to Work with the School

"My son had teachers who believed in him and challenged him, even if they had to change their teaching method to allow him to excel."

Parent of a sixth grader

"When the teachers and the psychologist and the nurse and the principal and all of those people on the child study team sit down with you and try to explain to you what's going on with your child, they use a lot of words you don't understand without explaining what they mean. You're intimidated because you're there with this big group of 'experts' so you just shake your head yes. You leave the meeting without having any idea of what's going on. You feel bad for your child, you feel bad for yourself, and you feel angry at everyone else."

Parent of a fourth grader

"There are many really good teachers. There are many teachers who have an excellent understanding of children who learn differently. But there are some teachers who teach one way and expect all of the kids to fit their mold. If they don't, there's something wrong with the kids."

Parent of a seventh grader

"My daughter has been blessed with a wonderfully supportive learning environment. Everyone from the speech therapist to the special education teacher, school psychologist, school counselor, teacher, and principal are 100% there for her."

Parent of a sixth grader

One of the most difficult tasks for parents of children with LD is striking a balance between cooperating with the school and advocating for their children. When your child is having trouble in school, you may wonder if you should ask for additional services or wait to see what happens next. When your child complains that another child is teasing him or her, or that a teacher is being unfair, you may feel torn between intervening or letting your child handle the situation. When a teacher complains about your child's behavior or lack of academic progress, you may ask yourself if the problem lies with the teacher or with your child. It's hard to know the right thing to do and when to do it.

Naturally, it's important to maintain a good relationship with the teachers, counselors, administrators, and others who are working with your child. But your primary concern should always be for your child. Is he receiving the best possible educational program? Is she getting all of the services she needs? This chapter offers some suggestions for addressing both issues—cooperating and advocating.

We both train teachers, counselors, and psychologists to work in schools. Before that, we worked in schools ourselves. We know that most teachers and other school personnel genuinely like children and try to do the best job they possibly can. However, as is true with any other group of people, there are different levels of experience, competence, and commitment among educators. Also, given the tremendous societal and financial challenges schools face today, some educators have become disillusioned. Therefore, it's possible that your child may encounter a teacher, administrator, or other staff person who is not doing a very good job. In that case, you are justified in expressing your concerns to the appropriate people in your school and school district. We believe that such educators are the exception, not the rule.

Even when the educators in your child's school are experienced, competent, and committed, you may find that some don't know much about LD. You may find yourself in the position of teaching a teacher, administrator, speech therapist, or psychologist about LD and what it means. Doing this tactfully can help to forge a positive working relationship between you and the professionals who work with your child.

By reading this book, you're already showing that you're committed to helping your child. Following are some suggestions that we hope will make this easier for you.

Be Assertive

"Always ask questions. If you don't understand even one part of the conference or IEP, ask. If your child's needs are not being met, say something. If you want something done a particular way—for example, if you want your child's progress reports to be mailed home to you, not given to your child—then make sure this is written into the IEP."

Parent of a ninth grader

There are three approaches people use to try to get something they want. One rarely works. One works sometimes, but for a price you may not want to pay. One almost always works because it encourages cooperation and mutual respect.

Being Passive

You want your child to spend more time in the regular classroom. You go to the LD teacher and say, "What do you think of Billy's program?" You speak in a soft voice and avoid making eye contact with the teacher. The teacher has no way of knowing what you really want. The teacher says, "I think Billy's program is working well for him. He's making good progress in the resource room."

You feel frustrated and angry with yourself for not saying what you really meant to say. The teacher is confused; she can tell how you're feeling, but she doesn't know why.

Being Aggressive

Again, you want your child to spend more time in the regular classroom. You go to the LD teacher and say, "I want Billy in the regular classroom more, starting immediately. He's not learning anything in your room. If you don't change his program by Monday, I'm going straight to the superintendent." You speak in a loud voice and glare at the teacher. She says, "I'm sorry you feel that way, and I'll see what I can do."

You feel like you've won a battle, but you may be embarrassed by the tactics you used. The teacher works hard over the next few days to change your child's educational program, calling rush meetings with other school staff. From that point on, you feel that the teachers don't like you and, in fact, are a little afraid of you. You wonder if they are treating your child any differently. Meanwhile, you start getting reports that your child is acting out aggressively to get what he wants at school.

Being Assertive

Once more, you want your child to spend more time in the regular classroom. You go to the LD teacher and say, "I've been thinking about Billy's program, and I would like him to start spending a few more hours each week in his regular classroom. How can we work together to make this change?" You speak in a medium tone of voice, maintain eye contact with the teacher, and state what you want clearly and directly. The teacher says, "Let me get back to you in a few days. I'll watch Billy more closely than usual and see how he does. I'll also talk to his regular classroom teacher and get his opinion. Maybe we can all meet early next week and talk about how to proceed. This sounds like a good idea to me, but let's make sure that it's right for Billy."

It's likely that you have achieved your goal without alienating anyone. In fact, you have strengthened your positive relationship with the LD teacher. You are working together for the same purpose, and that feels good for both of you.

If you find it hard to be assertive, you're not alone. Many adults get tongue-tied when it comes to expressing their wants and needs. Do yourself a favor and take an assertiveness training class.

Check with your local parks and recreation department, YMCA/YWCA, community mental health center, or community college. Or read a book or two about assertiveness and practice the techniques the authors describe. Following are some titles we know and recommend:

▶ *Asserting Yourself: A Practical Guide for Positive Change* by S. Bower (Reading, MA: Addison-Wesley, 1991).

▶ *Feel the Fear and Do It Anyway* by S. Jeffers (New York: Fawcett Columbine, 1988).

▶ *Overcoming Indecisiveness: The Eight Stages of Effective Decision-Making* by T. Rubin (New York: Avon Books, 1986).

▶ *When I Say No, I Feel Guilty* by M. Smith (New York: Bantam, 1985).

▶ *Your Perfect Right: A Guide to Assertive Living,* 6th ed., by R. Alberti and M.L. Emmons (San Luis Obispo, CA: Impact Publishers, 1990).

Teach Your Child to Be Assertive and Handle Conflicts

There will be times when your child has conflicts with other children or with a teacher. Like many parents, you'll probably want to run to the rescue. Depending on the circumstances and your child's age and social skills, it may be best for you to intervene. Eventually, however, children need to start solving their own problems. You can help your child by teaching him or her some basic assertiveness skills.

In *The School Survival Guide for Kids with LD*, we offer the following suggestions on how to be assertive. Share them with your child, and practice them in role plays until your child begins to feel comfortable using them.

▶ Talk in a medium tone of voice, not too loud and not too soft.

▶ Look the other person in the eye. Do not look at your shoes or the sky.

▶ Make suggestions. Do not make demands.

▶ If you do not get what you want, thank the person for listening. Try again another time. Do not make threats.

Being assertive is an important part of handling conflicts effectively. All children have difficulties getting along with others, but some children with LD seem to have more than their share, perhaps because they are so often frustrated with their schoolwork. In *The School Survival Guide for Kids with LD*, we outline a seven-step process for conflict resolution. As with the suggestions for assertiveness given above, we recommend that you discuss each step with your child and practice role-playing some possible scenarios.

1. **Tell the other person how you see the problem.** Use an I-message. An I-message has three parts: "I feel..." "...when you..." "...because...." Tell how you feel. Tell what the other person is doing to cause the conflict or keep it going. Tell how the conflict is affecting you.

2. **Listen to what the other person has to say about the problem.** Listen carefully even if you don't like what the other person is saying, and even if you think the other person is wrong. Don't interrupt while the other person is talking.

3. **Repeat what the other person thinks the problem is.** Then repeat what you think the problem is. Then ask, "What should we do?"

4. **Work together to brainstorm ways to solve the problem.** In brainstorming, everybody tries to come up with as many ideas as they can. All ideas are okay during brainstorming. Nobody makes fun of anybody else's ideas. It will help if someone makes a list of the brainstormed ideas so you are sure to remember them all.

5. **Decide on a solution.** Look at the list of brainstormed ideas. Work together to decide on the best one. You both have to agree on which idea to try.

6. **Decide how to do it.** Work together to agree on a way to put your solution into action.

7. **Decide if it works.** Evaluate your solution. Study it and think about it. Did it solve the problem? Did it solve only part of the problem? Did it make the problem worse? If the solution you tried didn't work, agree to try another solution.

The more familiar your child becomes with these assertiveness and conflict-resolution skills, and the more comfortable your child feels about using them, the less you will need to go to school to take care of problems for your child.

You may want to encourage your child to read a book about assertiveness. Here is a suggestion:

▶ *How to Say No and Keep Your Friends* by S. Scott (Amherst, MA: Human Resource Development, 1986). For young people in grades 6–12.

Avoid Blaming

"I feel very angry at the school system. I was relying
on professionals to help me through this. They didn't
do anything for my child. They could have been
more creative, but they weren't."

Parent of an eighth grader

Over the years, you may be frustrated with your child's school performance and academic progress. You may feel this way once in a while, often, or all the time. You will want to make sure to stay informed about your child's school program and to speak up any-time you believe that changes should be made. But even when you do everything "right," it may not be reasonable to expect that your child will overcome all of his or her school difficulties.

Sometimes it may seem that your child's lack of school progress is the fault of a particular teacher or a certain teaching method. In our experience, it is *never* helpful to blame a teacher for a child's learning difficulties. This puts the teacher on the defensive and creates hard feelings all around. See if there isn't another way to approach the situation.

For example: Your child is not meeting the goals set forth on his IEP. Rather than trying to figure out whose fault this is, and rather than blaming the teacher, maybe it's time to look more carefully at the IEP itself. We find that school personnel can be overly optimistic about the amount of progress they expect a child to make during the year. You might want to ask for more realistic goals on the IEP.

Know Your Rights

"If I was advising another parent, I would say, 'Get involved! Learn all you can.' I didn't, and I feel a lot of remorse today."

Parent of an adult with LD

In Chapters 4 and 5, we discuss the legal rights of children with LD and their parents. We strongly suggest that you thoroughly familiarize yourself with your rights—not so you can use them as threats if you are dissatisfied, but so you have a clear understanding of what to expect from your child's special education program.

For example, if you are unhappy with the evaluation of your child conducted by the school psychologist, it helps to know that you have the right to request an independent evaluation. You're not being a troublemaker; you're simply exercising your rights. Knowing your rights can help you to maintain a productive, cooperative relationship with the school.

Be a Reinforcer, Not a Teacher

Your child has a full load of work—and frustration—at school. The last thing your child needs is another full load at home. What can you do to help? Show interest and listen when your child tells you about her day. Look over any schoolwork she brings home and offer assistance when she needs it (and asks for it). Always be sure to praise and encourage your child's accomplishments and efforts.

Some teachers may ask you to do some specific activities with your child at home. This is fine, as long as you and your child are comfortable and enjoy doing the activities together. However, if this results in conflict between you and your child, we suggest that you reduce or avoid such activities. Talk to the teacher and find out if there are alternatives to at-home projects that require your involvement.

Allow Your Child to Experience Consequences

Children with LD have to deal with so much frustration and so many everyday problems that it's tempting to want to shield them from the consequences of poor choices. This doesn't help them. In fact, it has the opposite effect. It teaches them that they are not responsible for their own behavior.

We worked with a boy named Gunther who often had difficulty completing his homework on time. One day, his teacher announced that the class would be taking a field trip in two weeks. To be allowed to go on the field trip, the students would have to complete 90 percent of their homework assignments on time. Gunther kept putting off doing his homework. The week before the field trip, he came down with the flu and missed three days of school. His mother convinced the teacher to let Gunther go on the field trip anyway. After that, it was very difficult to get Gunther to do any of his homework on time. He had learned that his mother would intervene when he was facing unpleasant consequences.

It isn't "mean" to insist that your child accept responsibility for his or her behavior. It's essential. Remember that your child will be an adult before too many years have passed. You won't always be there to intervene, and it's never too soon to start experiencing logical consequences.

Work Together to Address Behavior Issues

"When a teacher calls to tell you that your child is having a problem—or your child is a problem—it's easy to think, 'What can I do? After all, something is wrong with my child.' Instead, push back your fears and negative thoughts. Start thinking about what you can do to help."

Parent of a ninth grader

No parent enjoys hearing that his or her child has gotten into trouble at school. In most cases, school personnel will want to work with you to come up with ways to manage your child's behavior.

Tell the school personnel that you'll talk to your child about the situation as soon as possible—that day, in fact, unless there's some compelling reason to wait. Hear what your child has to say. Then call the school and request a meeting. Everyone who works with your child should be there—the regular classroom teacher, LD teacher, school counselor, school social worker, school psychologist, and other specialists. The purpose of the meeting is not to blame others or to accept blame, but to work together on an action plan to address your child's behavior.

At the meeting, examine any and all factors which might be contributing to your child's behavior. Examples: the curriculum (is it appropriate?), the teaching methods (do they need modification?), your child's self-concept, any issues at home that might be affecting your child's school behavior, how the child feels about his or her LD and school program, and any emotional or social difficulties the child might be having.

Make it clear that you want to keep the lines of communication open between you and the school until the situation has been resolved. Then let your child know that you and the school are working together to help him or her through a difficult time.

11

Getting Help Outside of School

While your child is growing up, you will probably hear of many "treatments" for LD. In a sincere effort to help your child, you may spend a lot of time and money pursuing these treatments. There is nothing wrong with your desire to help your child, but there are certain issues you should consider before taking your child to a practitioner outside of the school.

Five Cautions

1. **As we explained in Chapter 1, there are at least five different types of LD, and these types can exist in many combinations.** Someone who claims to "cure" LD, or who works with all children with learning differences in the same way, either doesn't understand LD or is misleading people.

2. **You may decide to pursue a particular treatment because a friend told you that it worked for his or her child.** But even if you see for yourself that the child seems to be improving, this doesn't necessarily mean that the same treatment will be effective for your child. Children with LD are unique individuals— just like all other children.

3. **Some treatments work because the people involved believe they will work.** Everyone—parents, teachers, the child— becomes enthusiastic, motivated, and actively involved. It's natural to get excited about a plan to help your child. However, be aware that this may divert your time and energy from more effective and realistic interventions.

   Gary once worked with the parents of a third grader with LD. The child had several academic difficulties and had not yet learned to read. The parents were angry and hostile toward the school and would not accept suggestions for working with their son at home. In the middle of the school year, they told Gary that their child would be leaving school an hour early each day to work on a "neurological patterning" program. For six hours a day, seven days a week, they would be helping their son with a series of exercises designed to shape his motor movements.

They had been told that if they followed this program faithfully, their son would be doing algebra in six months.

Although the child showed some improvement in his academic performance, he never came anywhere near achieving the gains his parents had been promised. In fact, it's likely that the gains he made were due more to the extra attention he was receiving—and his parents' belief in the program—than to the program itself. Also, he had been hearing for years what a terrible job the school was doing. When parents have a negative attitude toward school, it's no surprise when their children perform poorly in school.

4. **If you go from practitioner to practitioner and from clinic to clinic in the hope of finding an effective treatment for your child's LD, your child may come to believe that there is something "wrong" with him or her that needs "fixing."** Eventually your child may think, "Things must be *really* serious if we have to see this many doctors." The child starts feeling learning *disabled* rather than learning different.

5. **If you find a practitioner whose methods and approach seem promising to you, do some "detective work" before you start treatment.** In most cases, there will be people at your child's school—the school psychologist, speech therapist, or LD teacher, for example—who will know about the various practitioners in your community and be familiar with their work. Or, if you are uncomfortable discussing this with school personnel, you might contact the special education department at a college or university in your area. A professor there might be able to point you toward readings or research in the area you are considering.

If the practitioner you are considering is licensed to practice by your state, contact the licensing board and ask if there have been any complaints about him or her. If the practitioner is not licensed, find out why.

Services Available in the Community

Psychologists

Generally, parents may contact a psychologist for testing, counseling, or both. We'll discuss testing here and counseling below, under mental health practitioners.

You may want a psychologist in private practice to test your child because you are unhappy with the evaluation you received from the school district, or because you want a second opinion. As explained in Chapter 5, you have the right to request an independent evaluation. In choosing a psychologist, you should be sure that the individual is licensed to practice psychology in your state and has an educational psychology or school psychology background. There are also some clinical psychologists who specialize in LD. Be sure to ask anyone you contact about his or her training and experience in working with children with LD.

Mental Health Practitioners

Psychiatrists, psychologists, social workers, counselors, and marriage and family therapists are the individuals in most states who provide counseling or psychotherapy services. State licensing laws vary, and you should make sure that the person you are considering is licensed in your state to practice privately. Or, if you go to a clinic, the person must be supervised by a licensed practitioner.

While you may pursue mental health services for a variety of home and/or school issues, you should determine if the person you intend to see is familiar with LD and has some knowledge regarding the relationship of LD to social and emotional difficulties.

Speech Therapists

If you feel that the school is unable or unwilling to provide adequate speech therapy for your child, you may elect to take your child to a private speech therapist. Again, make sure that the individual is licensed to provide such services in your state. Ask about his or her prior experience with children with LD. It's usually a good sign if he or she has worked in the schools.

While additional speech and language work may benefit your child, you should not confuse this with academic assistance. There is a relationship between language and academics, but it is not a given that your child's academic skills will improve as a result of speech therapy.

Physical Therapists

You may choose to see a private physical therapist if you are unable to obtain this service through the school, or if you are unhappy with the services provided. Physical therapy has been proven helpful for children with motor difficulties; in some cases, sensory motor integration has been linked to an improvement in learning.

Learning Centers and Tutors

Parents often ask us about the advisability of providing their child with extra academic assistance outside of school. Learning centers and tutors who understand LD and can adapt their methods and materials to the different types of LD may be useful for some children under some circumstances. Keep in mind that if your child is struggling academically and feeling depressed about school, more academic work may be the *last* thing he or she wants or needs.

It's important that children perceive a learning center or sessions with a tutor as helpful and enjoyable. Some children who start with a negative attitude may be positively influenced by an inspiring, motivating teacher and interesting curricula. If you choose to get extra academic help for your child, we encourage you to closely monitor the situation. Make sure that it doesn't turn into yet another "failure" experience for your child.

Optometrists

Some developmental optometrists provide visual training treatment for children. While such treatment may help a child with a visual impairment, there is no research indicating that it can lead to improved academic performance in reading. However, if you have any reason to think that your child might have trouble seeing or focusing, you should certainly have your child examined by a qualified pediatric optometrist.

Chiropractors

Some chiropractors have claimed that adjustments can remedy any number of maladies and conditions, including LD. Again, there is no research which supports chiropractic treatment as a "cure" for LD.

Nutritionists

Naturally, your child's diet should be healthful, and if you have any reason to believe that your child is suffering from food allergies, it is certainly advisable to check it out. Children who don't get the proper nutrition tire easily and have difficulty concentrating in school, which can certainly affect their school performance. However, research does not support the idea that changes in diet will "cure" a child's LD. When a child's academic performance improves after a change in diet, it is probably because he or she has more energy and is better able to concentrate.

If you have any questions or doubts about your child's diet, then you probably should consult your physician or a qualified nutritionist. However, it is unrealistic to expect that changing your child's diet—for example, by removing sugar or adding fish—will have any significant effect on his or her learning differences.

12

Looking toward the Future: Getting Ready to Let Go

Four Case Studies

Jessica

Twenty-six-year-old Jessica has a winning smile and an engaging personality. People who meet her don't know that she has LD unless she chooses to tell them. Currently Jessica lives by herself in an apartment and works 10–20 hours per week at a day-care center. She has recently separated from her husband of three years and plans to get a divorce as soon as she can afford it. Her husband is unemployed and was physically abusive to her when they were together.

Her parents support Jessica's decision to end her marriage and are trying to help her get back on her feet. Since graduating from high school, Jessica has had many jobs, most in day-care centers, but she has never worked longer than six months at any job. She has been fired from most jobs she has had, usually because of her "no-call-no-show" behavior. She doesn't drive, she rarely cooks for herself, and she continues to depend on her parents for emotional and financial support.

Bruce

Bruce, like Jessica, is 26. He has a speech difficulty that interferes with his ability to communicate effectively and clearly, especially when he is tired or excited. He has never married and doesn't date, although he does have female friends. He lives alone in an apartment and can cook for himself, but he prefers to eat fast food.

Since finishing high school, Bruce has worked steadily in grocery stores and warehouses. He has changed jobs only four times—twice when he moved to a different city, once when he was laid off during an economic downturn, and once when he got a better offer. Every time he has left a job, his employers have given him excellent letters of recommendation. These aren't always enough to convince employers who are put off by Bruce's speech difficulty and assume that he's retarded. However, Bruce is very persistent, and employers who take a chance on him are never sorry because he is such a capable and dependable worker.

Bruce drives his own car, manages his own money (except during emergencies, when his parents offer short-term assistance), and demands his independence.

Tony

Tony is 30, articulate, and attractive. He is also bright; over the years, his IQ test scores have ranged anywhere from 125 to 140. He has been a college student for seven years and plans to graduate soon with a major in early childhood education.

College has been a struggle for Tony, who has a severe reading disability; he can read words, but he can't remember anything he reads. Fortunately, he attends a university that provides a great deal of support for students with LD, including tutoring, note-taking services, and professors who are educated about learning differences. The tuition is expensive, but Tony's parents are professionals and have been able to pay for his schooling.

Tony doesn't drive; he is highly distractible and worries that his lack of concentration may cause an accident.

We recently asked Tony if he thought the years he had spent in college had been worth it. After a long pause, he responded, "I'll think so after I graduate, but there are times when I wish that I never started." Since starting college, Tony has had almost no social life because of the time he has had to spend keeping up with his studies. "I never would have made it this far without support from my parents and the disabled student office," he says. "But now I can see the light at the end of the tunnel. I'm eager to graduate and start a job."

Sue

Sue is a graduate student, currently pursuing her doctoral degree in counseling. She already has two other graduate degrees. Sue's LD continues to affect her spelling and writing. Although she is very bright and works extremely hard, she must rely on the spellchecker in her computer and ask friends to proofread her written work. On essay tests, she still comes up with strange spellings. Sue's LD has been an obstacle to her educational goals, but through persistence, hard work, and intelligence, she is meeting her objectives.

Challenges and Changes: Ways to Help Shape Your Child's Future

All four of these young adults with LD are facing different kinds of challenges. Jessica is having difficulty attaining financial and personal independence. She has no trouble finding work, but she can't hold onto a job for any length of time. Bruce has excellent work habits and understands the value of hard work, but employers are reluctant to hire him because of his speech difficulty. Tony may never experience the independence that comes from being able to drive a car. And Sue will always struggle with her spelling abilities.

Together, these young people illustrate some common experiences of many adults with learning differences. Although Jessica, Bruce, Tony, and Sue are continuing to develop and mature, they may take longer to achieve full financial, personal, and emotional independence than adults who do not have LD. The extent to which each will experience success depends on a number of factors including personal motivation, persistence, and the amount of support and encouragement they continue to receive from their parents, employers, teachers, and friends.

For more stories about young people with LD, you may want to read this book:

▶ *Succeeding Against the Odds: Strategies and Insights from the Learning Disabled* by S.L. Smith (New York: Jeremy P. Tarcher, 1993).

Your child's future as an adult may still be many years away, but there are things you can do today to help your child become independent and successful. Whether your child is a teenager or a preschooler, average or gifted, struggling or coping, read on.

Be Realistic about Your Child's Strengths and Limitations

When you picture your child's future, what do you see? Do you have a particular goal in mind for him or her? Do your dreams for your child accurately reflect his or her personal strengths and limitations? The ability to be realistic about your child is a crucial indicator of how well you will be able to plan for your child's future and guide your child in a direction that is most likely to ensure success.

We hope that you will be open to considering many possible directions for your child. Don't let yourself become obsessed with a single vision. For example, most parents—including parents of children with LD—want their children to go to college and become successful professionals. But this may not happen exactly the way they want it to, and in some cases it may not happen at all.

When Rhoda learned that her son, Carter, had learning differences, the first question she asked the psychologist was, "Will he be able to go to college?" Of course, the psychologist couldn't answer; Carter was only four years old at the time. Rhoda soon discovered that raising a child with LD posed new challenges every day. Eventually she realized that the question of college was minor when compared with the need to make sure that Carter received the best educational and personal opportunities in grade school, middle school, and high school. Carter is 29 now and has not yet gone to college. However, he is independent, he is happy, and he is finding his own way. He is starting to talk about taking a class or two at the community college, but he warns Rhoda not to pressure him, insisting that he will enroll in classes if and when he feels he is ready! Rhoda feels comfortable with Carter's decision—and applauds his assertiveness and positive self-esteem.

We believe that some kind of post-secondary education is important for everyone, and we encourage you to think of college or a vocational-technical program as a possible goal for your child. Just be realistic and keep your child's strengths and limitations in mind. Larry Faas, a researcher at Arizona State University, has interviewed hundreds of college students with LD. He has found that while many eventually graduate, most were bright to begin with. Even so, it wasn't easy for them. They gave up a great deal in the process, and many have questioned whether their sacrifices were worth it.

Form a Parent Group

Problems are always easier to solve when they can be shared with others who are in the same situation. In many communities and most states, there is an organization especially for parents of children with LD. The Learning Disabilities Association (LDA, formerly the Association for Children with Learning Disabilities) has been a driving force behind many national laws and policies that have been enacted to protect the educational rights of children with learning differences.

The national executive board of the LDA and all state boards are made up of parents of children with LD. You may already belong to the LDA. If not, ask your school or the local United Way agency if such an organization exists in your community. If there is not a local LDA in your community, you may wish to start one. For information about organizing an LDA, write or call the national office:

Learning Disabilities Association (LDA)
4156 Library Road
Pittsburgh, PA 15234
(412) 341-1515.

If there is not a local LDA in your community and you are not interested in starting one yourself, you may wish to form an informal group of parents who have children with LD. Sometimes it helps to get together with other parents to share experiences, vent frustrations, and think of ways to improve local services for your children. If you would like to form a group but aren't sure how to find other parents, here are some suggestions you may find useful:

1. **Ask your local superintendent of schools or special education consultant if you may distribute an informational flier to LD teachers for children to take home to their parents.** The flier should include your reasons for wanting to start a group, a place for interested parents to write their names, addresses, and phone numbers, and your own name and phone number.

2. **Place an ad in the classifieds section of your local newspaper.** State your wish to start a group for parents of children with LD. Include your telephone number so interested parents can contact you.

3. **Ask your child's teacher for suggestions about the best way to contact parents.** The teacher can also put you in touch with other people who may be able to help you.

4. **Place announcements in your community.** Try the local grocery store bulletin boards, school district newsletters, and/or television and radio community service bulletins.

Organizing a parent group can be difficult and time-consuming, but it's worth the effort. A group is an excellent way for parents to come together to support one another and to collectively advocate for their children. If one parent requests special services for a child, school personnel may "take it under consideration." When a dozen parents request special services for their children, and they make their request as a group, school personnel are more likely to act. Similarly, lawmakers and social agencies are always more responsive to groups of concerned citizens than to individuals acting alone.

Stay Involved at the School Level

In Chapters 4 and 5, we describe the school-related rights that you and your child enjoy. Never, ever fear that you are being "a bother," "pushy," or "obnoxious" when you insist that these rights be honored. Always remember that the school district is bound by law to provide your child with the most appropriate educational program.

However, most school personnel are exceedingly busy, and special education teachers often are overburdened with the numbers of children they work with each day. They need all the help they can get, and they usually welcome parents' input and support.

Be sure to attend your child's IEP meeting each year. Check to see that the educational program includes goals and objectives that relate to vocational and social needs as well as academic needs. If these goals and objectives are absent, ask that they be written into the IEP. We believe that vocational and social goals and objectives should start being part of a child's IEP as early as the first grade. They *must* be addressed no later than sixth or seventh grade.

Even if you think that your child will probably attend college, instruction in vocational and social skills is still important. If your child doesn't attend college, those skills will make it easier to find a full-time job after high school.

Provide Your Child with Early Work Experiences

"I believe that my daughter has the ability to support herself and take care of herself in the future. My hope is that she'll find a career she'll enjoy and can succeed at. There are some areas in which she does well. Hopefully she'll be able to capitalize on those. I'm not sure where her skills will fit in, but we're going to do everything we can to help her capture her strengths."

Parent of a ninth grader

Early work experiences are valuable for all children, including those with learning differences. Even children in grade school can run errands for neighbors or take care of their plants and pets when they are out of town.

Middle-school students can baby-sit, do yard work, or get a paper route. A paper route especially demands responsibility and forces a young person to accomplish the same tasks at the same time on a daily basis—and start forming reliable work habits.

We know that early work experiences help to prepare young people for more difficult jobs and greater responsibilities in the future. We're convinced that they are an important factor in a young person's success as an adult. Further, we believe that adolescents with LD should get real jobs while they are still in high school. However, they should not work more than 10–15 hours per week—20 at the most. Some research suggests that high school students who work more than 10–15 hours per week are more likely to have difficulties with their school work and suffer from a lack of social interactions. For students with LD, who are more likely than others to have trouble with school and relationships, limiting work hours can be especially important.

If you want your child to have work experience, but you are concerned that his or her schoolwork will suffer, we suggest that you allow your child to work during the summer but not while school is in session.

You may want to encourage your child to take a career assessment, which usually involves special tests called "work interest inventories." A work interest inventory gives the test-taker valuable insights into his or her personality, likes and dislikes, and work interests, then describes jobs that are likely to be a good match. One of the best work interest inventories is *The Self-Directed Search (SDS)*. Developed by John Holland, it is appropriate for teenagers who are 14 and older. Also available, but easier to read: *The Self-Directed Search, Form Easy (SDS-E)*. For more information, write or call:

Psychological Assessment Resources, Inc.
P.O. Box 998
Odessa, FL 33556
Toll-free telephone: 1-800-331-8378

To find out about other work interest inventories, talk to the LD teacher or school counselor.

Encourage Your Child to Volunteer

Volunteer work makes us feel good about ourselves. It also puts our problems in perspective. There are many people whose problems are far more severe than our own. When we help them, we help ourselves.

Children with LD who get involved in volunteer work realize many benefits from the experience: a boost in their self-esteem, the awareness that they are not the only people with difficulties, and practice at being good citizens.

Younger children may be encouraged to help out elderly neighbors by putting their morning newspaper on the porch each day or by feeding the pet of a friend who is out of town. Older children and adolescents can volunteer to work with service agencies, answering telephones or addressing envelopes.

Paid work teaches young people good work habits and how to manage their money. Volunteer work teaches them about the importance of putting other people first. Both kinds of work build character and responsibility.

For true stories about young people who are making a difference in the world, many by doing volunteer work, we recommend these books:

▶ *Kids with Courage* by B.A. Lewis (Free Spirit Publishing, 1992).

▶ *Kidstories: Biographies of 20 Young People You'd Like to Know* by J. Delisle (Free Spirit Publishing, 1991).

For ideas on how and where to volunteer, try these books:

▶ *150 Ways Teens Can Make a Difference: A Handbook for Action* by M. Salzman, T. Reisgeis, and Thousands of Teenage Contributors (Princeton, NJ: Peterson's Guides, 1991).

▶ *The Kid's Guide to Service Projects: Over 500 Service Ideas for Young People Who Want to Make a Difference* by B.A. Lewis (Free Spirit Publishing, 1995).

Learn about Your Community's Resources and Social Services while Your Child is Still in School

Many communities provide resources and social assistance to individuals with disabilities, both while they are in school and after they graduate. Find out what resources are available in your community and in your state that can help prepare your child for life as an adult.

Begin by calling or visiting your local United Way or Community Services organizations. These agencies usually have brochures or pamphlets that describe the purpose and function of most community services. Find out about those services that apply to your child's needs. Call the agencies or visit in person, and ask them to explain their services to you.

In Chapter 4, we describe the Individualized Transition Plan (ITP), a document that includes specific goals and objectives for preparing your child for life after high school. If you would like the services of a particular community agency to be provided while your child is still in school, make sure to include this request in your child's ITP. For example, your child may be eligible to work in a state-supported job opportunities program that will pay his or her salary for summer work in a city, county, or state job. If this is an opportunity you want for your child, discuss it in the annual IEP meeting and ask that it be listed as a specific transition goal.

Don't Feel Sorry for Your Child

In Chapter 9, we advise you not to overprotect or overindulge your child, but instead to allow your child to experience the consequences of his or her choices and behaviors. We can't emphasize how important it is for your child to learn to carry his or her own weight—learning that doesn't come easily.

We all love our children, and we want to protect them from potentially unpleasant and hurtful experiences. However, we sometimes carry this concern too far. We do everything for our children except give them the chance to stop needing us so much

Just like the rest of us, children with LD learn from their experiences. Also like the rest of us, they tend to learn the most from their negative experiences. While we would never suggest that you deliberately arrange bad experiences for your child, or that you not step in when your child is in real danger, we feel that too much parental concern prevents children from growing up and becoming independent.

Let Go When the Time Comes

◻◼◻◼◻◼◻◼◻◼◻◼◻◼◻◼◻◼◻◼◻◻

"When your is born, you have all of these hopes and dreams—that your child is going to be one of the best, get along with everybody, be respected, have good self-esteem, be smart, do wonderful things, and have a glorious career. It's hard to understand that your child is not going to be above average or even average in a lot of things. But once you come to grips with this, once you accept your child, it gives you a kind of peace. And you don't have to stop hoping and dreaming."

Parent of a twelfth grader

◻◼◻◼◻◼◻◼◻◼◻◼◻◼◻◼◻◼◻◼◻◻

All children, with or without LD, eventually grow into adolescents and start demanding their independence. This is perfectly normal. So is our reaction as parents: resisting this transition and trying to hold onto our children for as long as we can.

Letting go can be almost unbearably hard. We worry that our children's peers will take advantage of them. We fear that if they learn to drive, they will kill themselves. We agonize over the possibility that they will do anything to have friends and won't have the courage to resist the pressure to do drugs or become sexually active.

These concerns are common to all parents of adolescents, but they can become all-consuming for parents of children with learning differences. We know that our children are more vulnerable than others and more likely to make decisions based on poor judgment, peer pressure, and manipulation by others. We are terrified every time they leave the house that they will suffer the dangerous, perhaps even fatal consequences of an uninformed choice or a naive behavior. What if they can't read important instructions? If they are easily distracted, how can they cross the street? What if they stumble and fall while getting on a bus or a subway car?

If they misread a stranger's social signals, will they provoke a hostile or even violent response?

As close as we want to keep our children, there comes a time when we can't hold them any longer. Sooner or later, your child will have to make some hard choices. In the process, he or she will stumble and fall a few times. If you leave room for your child to have these experiences now, while you're still around to offer support and encouragement, then he or she is more likely to get up and try again.

If you want your child to become an independent adult tomorrow, then back off a little today. Let your child decide what clothes to wear, what hairstyle to try, whether to live in a messy room. Encourage your teenager to learn to drive, find a job, and start dating. Your son or daughter needs the same freedoms and privileges other young people have. So...start letting go.

Resources

SAMPLE INDIVIDUALIZED
EDUCATION PROGRAM (IEP)

IEP TEAM

Student: Kelly R.

Parent(s): Mr. and Mrs. R.

Teachers: Ms. Brown (voc. ed.)

Mr. Jones (sp. ed.)

Mrs. Turner (rd. spec.)

Agency Representative: Ms. Jones

(principal)

Others:

STUDENT INFORMATION

D.O.B.: 6/2/78 Age:16 Grade:10

Phone: 555-4162

Address: 12 Holly Court

Anytown, USA 99999

School: West View High School

****

PROCEDURAL CHECKLIST

	DATE
Written notice about program initiation/change	11/20/94
Consent for preplacement evaluation	9/20/90
Consent for initial placement	9/28/90

Special Education and Related Services to be Provided	Persons Responsible	Date Initiated	Duration
remedial reading and math/daily	Turner/Stone	12-01-94	review IEP
vocational education—in-class help 3 times weekly	Brown	12-01-94	5-10-95
tutorial help in social studies & science; lab assistance	Jones	12-03-94	
special class in basic skills—one hour weekly	Jones	12-08-94	
biweekly consultation with 4 core subject area teachers	Jones	11-11-94	

EXTENT OF TIME IN REGULAR EDUCATION
PROGRAM 80% in regular classes and 20% in remedial classes

★★★★★★★★★★★★★★★★
EVALUATION DATA

WISC-R (10-93) Verbal—68, Performance—72, Full Scale—70

PIAT (10-93) Math—6.7, Word Recognition—4.4,
Comprehension—4.0, Spelling—4.8, Total—5.0

WRAT (10-93) Math—6.9, Reading—4.6, Spelling—5.0

Vineland Social Maturity Scale (10-93) Age Equivalent: 12—8,
Chronological Age 16—4

Modality Preference Testing Procedure (10—80) Visual Mode

(continued next page)

Present Levels of Performance	Annual Goals	Instructional Objectives	Evaluation Procedures
Comprehends at 4.0 level. Spells at 5.0 level.	Kelly will increase his reading to at least the 5.0 level and spelling to the 6.0 level. Kelly will increase his writing skills using occupational tasks.	Reading Lab: Given small-group instruction, Kelly will: Spell and define survival words typically found on a job application, and other vocationally related words. Write simple sentences and paragraphs correctly. Accurately complete such forms/letters as applications, registration forms, thank-you notes, want ad replies. Evaluate information in want ads. Communicate effectively on the telephone. Define abbreviations commonly used on application forms. Describe a resume verbally; list reasons for using a resume; write a resume for himself. List 5 elements of a successful interview; appropriately answer 10 sample interview questions. Read high interest–low level books, selected by Kelly and approved by Mr. Turner, no less than 1 biweekly. Read a 15-minute daily assignment from the newspaper with an occupational emphasis in workbook.	80% accuracy expected on all daily assignments 85% accuracy expected on all teacher-made weekly quizzes Woodcock Reading Mastery Tests will be used to test achievement semi-annually

Present Levels of Performance	Annual Goals	Instructional Objectives	Evaluation Procedures
Reads, writes, and interprets correctly numerical information, cardinal and ordinal numbers. Progressing in subtracting decimals (math skills at 6.7 level). Uses calculator for most computation.	Kelly will increase his quantitative and numerical skills to at least a productive level (70–80% accuracy).	Math Lab: In an individualized math lab, Kelly will: Discriminate among different sizes, shapes, textures. Define and correctly use such common numbers as ZIP codes, phone numbers, social security numbers. Estimate distances, sizes, and weights accurately. Correctly measure perimeter, weight, time, temperature.	All objectives will be checked on the following scale through weekly quizzes: Unfamiliar Introduced Progressing 50–70% success Productive 70–85% success Competent 85–100% success
	Kelly will attain basic money management skills at a competent level (85–100% accuracy).	List common financial responsibilities and describe how to accommodate each; include obligations and luxuries. Discuss principles of banking; include credit, loans, savings. Match common coins/bills with their correct names. Accurately make change using up to $100. Distinguish between gross and net pay. Write sample checks correctly, balance checkbook. Fill in and compute time cards. Prepare biweekly and monthly budgets—data furnished.	The Key Math Test will be used to test achievement semi-annually.

(continued next page)

Present Levels of Performance	Annual Goals	Instructional Objectives	Evaluation Procedures
No work experience using basic principles.	Kelly will attain pre-employment skills at an employable level including an understanding of:	Job Skills: Given the requisite materials, tools, equipment, and training, Kelly will:	Participation in class discussions and work sample activities.
	the free enterprise system	Compare/contrast the American private enterprise system with other economic systems. Discuss investment opportunities, competition, automation, specialization, taxation. List the influences of labor organizations on the economy, business, and individuals. Name 5 reasons that demonstrate the value of work.	Observation, oral and written quizzes. Biweekly check scale used for all objectives through oral and written assessment:
	work possibilities and basic principles	Explore various jobs and occupational clusters. Demonstrate a working knowledge of basic mechanical principles (e.g. levers, screws, pulleys, vacuums).	Unfamiliar Maintaining Progressing 50–70% success
	good work habits	List characteristics and abilities, attitudes, and habits of successful workers. Maintain appropriate hygiene and dress. Be on time consistently and accept consequences for tardiness. Work dependably and independently without direct, continuous supervision. Demonstrate concern for/adherence to safety precautions.	Productive 70–80% success Employable 85–100% success

Present Levels of Performance	Annual Goals	Instructional Objectives	Evaluation Procedures
About a 4th grade reading level and weak in technical vocabulary. Strong in spelling, with good dictionary skills (5.0 level).	occupational communications.	Read and follow written instructions correctly (e.g. labels, procedural manuals, street signs). Define and correctly use technical vocabulary at a level sufficient for work experience communication.	
As determined by a work sample inventory, Kelly's manual dexterity is not age-appropriate (about 4 years behind).	Kelly will improve his manual dexterity.	Coordinate hand-eye-foot movements accurately. Coordinate the use of both hands effectively, including lifting, turning, pulling, placing, and using small hand tools and equipment. Demonstrate effective finger agility.	Monthly work sample assessment and successful completion of work sample kit activities as determined by teacher observation.

Books for Children and Teenagers

▶ Aiello, B., and Shulman, J., *Secrets Aren't (Always) for Keeps* (Frederick, MD: Twenty-First Century Books, 1988). After successfully hiding her learning differences from her Australian pen pal, Jennifer becomes worried when her pen pal announces she is coming for a visit and she wants to spend a day at Jennifer's school.

▶ Caple, K., *The Biggest Nose* (Boston, MA: Houghton Mifflin, 1985). Eleanor Elephant is taunted by the other animal children for having the biggest nose in the group, and she is embarrassed to find out that it is true. When Eleanor tries to shorten her nose, she learns it is good just the way it is. Again confronted, Eleanor finds a way to stop the teasing.

▶ Giff, P.R., *Today Was a Terrible Day* (New York: Puffin Books, 1984). Ronald's day goes from bad to worse. He accidentally squirts water on Joy, drops Miss Tyler's plant, misses the ball during recess, and is teased for his lack of reading ability. Also available on audio cassette.

▶ Gilson, J., *Do Bananas Chew Gum?* (New York: Simon & Schuster Trade, 1989). Able to read and write at only a second grade level, sixth grader Sam Mott considers himself dumb until he is prompted to cooperate with those who think something can be done about his problem.

▶ Greenwald, S., *Will the Real Gertrude Hollings Please Stand Up?* (New York: Dell, 1985). Gertrude, an eleven-year-old girl with learning differences, spends several weeks with an overachieving cousin. They both learn a lot about themselves and the limitations labels can impose.

▶ Janover, C., *Josh, A Boy with Dyslexia* (Burlington, VT: Waterfront Books, 1988). Josh Grant and his family have difficulty dealing with his learning differences. He struggles to fit in with his peers and feel an accepted part of his new school.

▶ Janover, C., *The Worst Speller in Jr. High* (Minneapolis: Free Spirit Publishing Inc., 1995). Katie must choose between Spud, a popular, handsome boy, and Brian, a "brain," while dealing with seventh grade, her mother's illness, and her own reading difficulty.

▶ Kraus, R., *Leo the Late Bloomer* (New York: HarperCollins Children's Books, 1994). Leo, the tiger, had difficulty with everything, from talking and eating to reading and writing. Leo's father was very worried. But both he and Leo learned the meaning of the word patience.

▶ Sharmat, M., *I'm Terrific* (New York: Holiday House, 1992). Jason Bear thinks his admirable traits make him terrific and tells all of his peers so. When his self-admiration is not reinforced, Jason becomes sloppy and is nasty to his friends. Unhappy with his own behavior, Jason finally learns that happiness comes from accepting himself.

~~~~~~~~~~~~~~~~~~~~~~~~~~~~~

More Books for Young Readers

▶ Alexander, H., *Look Inside Your Brain* (New York: Grosset & Dunlap, 1991).

▶ Dwyer, K., *What Do You Mean, I Have a Learning Disability?* (New York: Walker and Company, 1991).

▶ Gehret, J., *The Don't-Give-Up Kid and Learning Differences* (Fairport, NY: Verbal Images Press, 1992).

▶ Giff, P.R., *The Beast in Ms. Rooney's Room* (New York: Dell-Yearling, 1984).

▶ Kline, S., *Herbie Jones* (New York: Puffin Books, 1986).

▶ Lasker, J., *He's My Brother* (Chicago: Albert Whitman, 1974).

▶ Minnetonka Public Schools, *If They Can Do It, We Can Too* (Minneapolis: Deaconess Press, 1992).

▶ Puckett, K., and Brown, G., *Be the Best You Can Be* (Minneapolis: Waldman House Press, 1993).

▶ Sanford, D., *Don't Look at Me* (Sisters, OR: Questar Publishers, 1986).

▶ Sheehan, P., *Kylie's Song* (Santa Barbara, CA: Advocacy Press, 1988).

▶ Simon, S., *Vulture: A Modern Allegory on the Art of Putting Oneself Down* (Sunderland, MA: Values Press, 1991).

▶ Waber, B., *"You Look Ridiculous," Said the Rhinoceros to the Hippopotamus* (Boston: Houghton Mifflin, 1979).

~~~~~~~~~~~~~~~~

Books about Career and College Planning

▶ The Careers Without College series includes titles on *Cars, Computers, Emergencies, Fashion, Fitness, Health Care, Kids,* and *Music* (Princeton, NJ: Peterson's).

▶ Fielding, P.M., and Moss, J.R., *National Directory of Four-Year Colleges, Two-Year Colleges, and Post High School Training Programs for Young People with Learning Disabilities,* 7th edition (1994: Partners in Publishing, Box 50347, Tulsa, OK 74150; telephone 918-835-8258).

▶ Lipkin, M., *Guide to Colleges with Programs or Services for Students with Learning Disabilities* (1990: Schoolsearch Press, 127 Marsh St., Belmont, MA 02178; telephone 617-489-5785).

▶ Mangrum, C.T., II, and Strichart, S.S., *Peterson's Guide to Colleges with Programs for Students with Learning Disabilities* (Princeton, NJ: Peterson's Guides, updated often).

▶ Scheiber, B., and Talpers, J., *Unlocking Potential: College and Other Choices for Learning Disabled People: A Step-by-Step Guide* (Bethesda, MD: Adler & Adler, 1987).

Organizations

CHADD
Children with Attention Deficit Disorder
499 NW 70th Avenue, Suite 109
Plantation, FL 33317
(305) 587-3700
Provides resources and support for parents of children with attention deficit disorder (ADD).

Council for Exceptional Children (CEC)
1920 Association Drive
Reston, VA 22091
(703) 620-3660
Dedicated to advancing the quality of education for all exceptional children and improving the conditions under which special educators work.

Learning Disabilities Association (LDA)
4156 Library Road
Pittsburgh, PA 15234
(412) 341-1515
Membership includes professionals and parents devoted to advancing the education and well-being of children and adults with learning disabilities. Contact the national organization for information on state and local chapters.

Marin Puzzle People, Inc.
17 Buena Vista Avenue
Mill Valley, CA 94941
(415) 383-8763
An organization of adults with learning disabilities. Publishes a monthly newsletter and a booklet to assist those who wish to start local clubs.

National Center for Learning Disabilities (NCLD)
381 Park Avenue South, Suite 1420
New York, NY 10016
(212) 545-7510
Promotes public awareness about learning disabilities, neurological disorders, and deficits which can be a barrier to literacy. Provides resources and referrals on a national level to a wide range of volunteers and professionals.

Index

About the Authors

 Gary Fisher, Ph.D., is a professor and director of the Addiction Training Center at the University of Nevada in Reno. He previously worked as a school psychologist in Washington State for ten years. Gary lives in Truckee, California, is married, and has two children, Colin and Aaron.

Rhoda Cummings, Ed.D., is a professor of special education at the University of Nevada in Reno. She lives in Reno and has two children, Carter and Courtney.

Gary and Rhoda are also the authors of *The Survival Guide for Kids with LD (Learning Differences)* (Free Spirit Publishing, 1990), *The School Survival Guide for Kids with LD (Learning Differences): Ways to Make Learning Easier and More Fun* (Free Spirit Publishing, 1991), and *The Survival Guide for Teenagers with LD (Learning Differences)* (Free Spirit Publishing, 1993).

In addition, Gary is co-author of *Substance Abuse: Information for Mental Health Professionals* (Needham Heights, MA: Allyn & Bacon, 1995), and Rhoda is the author of *Adolescence: A Developmental Perspective* (Orlando, FL: Harcourt Brace & Company, 1995).

MORE FREE SPIRIT BOOKS

The School Survival Guide for Kids with LD (Learning Differences):
Ways to Make Learning Easier and More Fun
by Rhoda Cummings, Ed.D., and Gary Fisher, Ph.D.
Kids learn how to organize their time, set goals, and stick up for themselves. "School tools" build confidence in reading, writing, spelling, math, and more. Special chapters tell how to handle conflict, stay out of trouble, cope with testing, and get help from adults.
$10.95; 176 pp.; illust.; s/c; 6" x 9"

The Survival Guide for Teenagers with LD (Learning Differences)
by Rhoda Cummings, Ed.D., and Gary Fisher, Ph.D.
Advice, information, and resources to help teenagers with LD succeed at school and prepare for life as adults. Topics include legal rights, advocating for yourself, getting a job, setting career goals, living on your own, dating and relationships, and more. Ages 13 and up. Also available on audio cassette.
$11.95; 200 pp.; illust.; s/c; 6" x 9"

How to Help Your Child with Homework: Every Caring Parent's Guide to Encouraging Good Study Habits and Ending the Homework Wars
by Marguerite Radencich, Ph.D., and Jeanne Shay Schumm, Ph.D.
Put an end to excuses and arguments while improving your child's school performance. Realistic strategies and proven techniques make homework hassle-free. Includes handouts, resources, and real-life examples. For parents of children ages 6-13.
$12.95; 208 pp.; illust.; s/c; 7 1/4" x 9 1/4"

The Survival Guide for Kids with LD (Learning Differences)
by Gary Fisher, Ph.D., and Rhoda Cummings, Ed.D.
Solid information and sound advice for children labeled "learning disabled." Explains LD in terms kids can understand, defines different kinds of LD, discusses LD programs, and emphasizes that kids with LD can be winners, too. Ages 8-12; reading level 2.7 (grade 2, 7th month). Also available on audio cassette.
$9.95; 104 pp.; illust.; s/c; 6" x 9"

Understanding LD (Learning Differences): A Curriculum to Promote LD Awareness, Self-Esteem, and Coping Skills in Students Ages 8-13
by Susan McMurchie
Based on Free Spirit's *Survival Guide for Kids with LD* and *School Survival Guide for Kids with LD,* this comprehensive curriculum of 23 lessons helps students with LD become more aware of their learning differences and more positive about their capabilities. Includes dozens of reproducible handouts.
$21.95; 160 pp.; s/c; 8 1/2" x 11"

School Power: Strategies for Succeeding in School
by Jeanne Shay Schumm, Ph.D., and Marguerite Radencich, Ph.D.
Covers getting organized, taking notes, studying smarter, writing better, following directions, handling homework, managing long-term assignments, and more. Ages 11 and up.
$11.95; 132 pp.; B&W photos and illust.; s/c; 8 1/2" x 11"

To place an order, or to request a free catalog of SELF-HELP FOR KIDS® materials, write or call:

Free Spirit Publishing Inc.
400 First Avenue North, Suite 616
Minneapolis, MN 55401-1730
toll-free (800)735-7323, local (612)338-2068